"NO GOLDEN AGERS HERE"

A HANDBOOK FOR PASTORS AND CHURCHES SERVING PEOPLE OVER 65 YEARS OF AGE

Blaine Taylor

"NO GOLDEN AGERS HERE"
A Handbook For Pastors and Churches Serving People Over 65 Years of Age
By Blaine Taylor

Edited by Janice Riddle and Steve Clapp

Printing and assembly by Crouse Printing of Champaign, Illinois. Special thanks to: David and Shirley Crouse, Steve Askins, Sonnie Schrock, Cheryl Bundy, Aimee Ward, Ralph Crabtree, Ed Anderson and Nan Craig.

This book is dedicated to those who have taught me over the years and whose love is reflected in these pages:

Ruth Berrett, Harry Hedenburg, Perry Howe, Win & Barbara Russell, Don & Rose Nelson, Roland & Eileen Sundberg, Emerson & Bea Wiggin, Alan Moore, Herbert & Ethel Langer, Polly Chaffee, Bill & June Spiller, Roy & Bev Paro, Frank & Pat Baril, Everett & Jean Berry, Wes & Shirley Broome, Spencer Gutridge, Arthur Bills, Hi & Mabel Gibbs, Ralph & Dot Ellis, Harry & Marion Rossland, George & Mary Richardson, Oscar Cook, Shaw Taylor, Rodney & Eva Hadley, Gene & Elenor Ellis, John & Joyce Sutherland, Bob & Dot Bunting, Evelyn & Jackson Burns, Bob & Madeline Cole, Ruth & Egidio Conti, Edwin S. Dahl, Norman Adams, Harrison Brown, Bardwell & Margaret Flower, Nelson & Mildred Spencer, Paul & Evelyn Goulding, Rosalie Benson, Frank & Velma Tattersall, Herbert & Elsie Kenworthy, Marilyn & John Bateman, Del & Doris Betterley, Claire & Ken Bicknell, Oliver Drake, Lem & Doris Lord, Les & Helen Burr, Bill & Dot Morgan, Helen Erickson, Farnham & Alice Goulding, Stan & Natalie Gutridge, Bill & Audrey Lewis, Harry & Vi Spencer, Ted & Betty Stoddard, Mel & Kay Thomas, Russ & Helen Phillips, Henri & Mildred Kokernak, Hughes Wagner, Gary Campbell, Margaret & George Benzie, Bob & Karin Bleakney, Glenn Glazier, Harold Cramer, Ed & Nancy Ross, Roger & Ruth Palmgren.

George & Mary Richardson, Lee & Alice Evans, Bessie Carty, Stanley & Margaret Barker, Lillie & Helen Almgren, Rosa Lee Adams, Dale & Jessie Fair, Merle & Frances Hall, Dora Hammond, Minnie Small, Grandma Doe, Homer Ginns, Ruth Fuller, Lois & Les Johnson, Will & Nan Ford, Roy & Margaret Hawes, Grace Horton, Francis Wilson, Elmo Young, Wilder & Gladys Smith, Al & Grace Tattersall, Leon & Margaret Treadwell, Bill & Alberta Pollock, Ken & Hilda Roper, Arline Scribner, Burt Walker, Henry & Katherine Williams, Sherman Clark, Marjorie Hirtle, Ed & Pricilla Mason, Wayne & Hazel Harlacher, Gladys & Ruth Hopkins, Clover Knowlton, Dick & Jane Thompson, Harold & Emma Jackson, Bob Jones, Barbara Jones Foley, Ed Foley, Hulda Karlson, Edith Bollinger, Carl & Ethel Swanberg, Eric & Inkie Swanberg, Alex & Clara Swanberg, Harry & Bertha Spencer, Sherman & Hazel Langille, Horatio Robbins, Guy Wayne, Ken & Roberta Grierson, Lizzie Goodnow, Bob & Margaret De Wallace, Myrtle & Fletcher Allen, Ralph Breen, Catherine Cudney, Fred & Ruth Scherr, Agnes Irish, Harold & Magdalene Hoyt, George Hunter, Ethel Spencer, Dorothy Anderson, Ed & Jane Holland.

Esther & Stan Salme, Carl Bartlett, Larry & Nita Beliveau, Kenneth & Elizabeth Berrett, Percy & Etta Betterley, Barry & Bea Bradshaw, Willard Brown, Mary Cunningham, Wilbur & Peggy Dahl, Ray & Dot Ewing, Ivar & Lilly Peterson, Fannie Cheney, Elsa Holmberg, Leroy & Lena Holden, Edna Hull, Fred & Adeline Holdsworth, Ed & Marion Green, Norman & Gladys Fralick, Ethel Churchill, Bob Bradlee, Al & Elizabeth Hodgkins, Elsie Haines, Alice Sawyer, Herbert & Florence Reed, Hank Rand, Hi & Hazel Phillips, Gordon & Evelyn Meisner, Wylie & Meredith Lantz, Elsie Laverty, Myrtle & Charles Allen, George Fallon, Ken & Audrey McMurtry, Mr. & Mrs. Charles Kirkpatrick, Ralph & Mary Williams, Willard Arnold, Newt Clay, Hilda Ogilvie, Christine Rose, Clarence Wormwood, Elissa Putukian, Bob & Alice Vannerson, Edson Waterhouse, Walter Muelder, Len & Pauline Akers, Eva Baker, Roy & Mildred Benson, Flora Bryant, Phyllis & Bernard Burns, Warren & Helen Davenport, Pauline & Ruth Dennis, Hubert Gallup, George & Ethel Holmberg, Mary Arslen, Roscoe & Edith Blunt, Ethel Ahearn, Inez Curtis, Lillian Nelson, Sam & Kathleen Spence, Stanley Wheeldon, Edith Gage, Dorothy & Ellen Fellows, Carl Fahnstrom, Stan & Winnie England, Herb & Barbara Dobie, Alden & Jean Liberty, Ernest & Ruth Lucas, Sandy & Edna Naylor, George & Florence Newton, Arthur & Louise Sjosten, Eric & Edith Segersten, Barbara Sperl, Jessie Speck, Tom & Mayaline Wallace, Forrest & Alice Bump, Georgia Corder, John Montgomery, Ira Roberts, Henry Bailey, Herbert Fulton, David & Shirley Skinner, Helen Russell, Ralph & Arline Quimby, Mae & John Rampsi, Ruth Catherwood, John & Millie Bushong, Ruth Fuller, Leona & Burchill Johnson, and so many others.

NO MATTER THE AGE

No matter the age —
It isn't the hour, the month, or the year,
Whatever the element of time that has passed
We think of all the things
We could have done
We could have changed.

No matter the age —
No one could tell us a thing
  when we were young.

No matter the age —
Our future has just begun.
It looms ahead like a darting,
  soaring, adventurous kite;
Trying us here, testing out there,
Tugging our dreams 'til with one we alight.

No matter the age —
No one can tell us what to do.
We must become pilot, navigator and crew.

No matter the age —
Time, like life, is ours to use:
It can't be borrowed or renewed.
It begins like a second, so very small
  grows, flourishes, matures:
age to ageless, all comes due.

Yet, no matter the age —
Would, we could, begin anew.

June K. Thomas
Gamma chapter
Alpha Kappa State
(Connecticut)
Published posthumously

CONTENTS

PREFACE

This is a handbook for pastors and churches trying to better serve those over sixty-five years of age. It is a tool-box of suggestions, illustrations and program suggestions designed for clergy and laypersons who are committed to ministry with America's fastest growing population group.

More than twenty-six million people in the United States are now over sixty-five years of age and another twenty-three million are in the fifty-four to sixty-four age group. More than 20% of the population is fifty-five years or older. Because of the post World War II baby boom, the percentage will continue to increase for the next thirty years.[1] If there are no substantial research breakthroughs concerning cancer and heart disease, there will be about thirty-one million people over sixty-five in the year 2000.[2] If a "cure" for either of these killer diseases is developed, or if research in slowing the aging process is fruitful, the figures given will be modest indeed.

Maggie Kuhn writes: "The percentage of church members over age sixty is at least twice as high as the general population."[3]

Already close to thirty percent of the active members of Christian churches in the United States are over sixty-five; however, many churches concentrate their ministries on other age groups. This book is an effort to encourage and enhance ministry through and for those over sixty-five. As the pastor for thirteen years of a large urban church, where over half of the active members were in this age group, I discovered that they were a remarkable resource. Many of my presuppositions about them were wrong because nothing in my college or seminary training had prepared me for such a ministry. In the very few times they were mentioned in seminary they were pictured as a problem group which needed special services.

In my urban parish I slowly began to learn something of what those over sixty-five had to teach me. I experienced their ministry. I observed their struggles and their needs. I discovered that they had strengths few of the rest of us recognized. And they had needs that I had never before considered. I had four kinds of relationships with those over sixty-five:

> **(1) As staff members.** In my years there, eleven different people, both lay and clergy, ranging from sixty-five to seventy-six years of age, were members of the church staff.

> **(2) As church members and constituents.** Half of the large congregation and an equal share of its leadership were over sixty-five. They were the key people in our mutual ministry.

vii

(3) As people in crisis and need. As does every other age group, those over sixty-five have special needs and often experience personal or family crises.

(4) As close friends. I learned so much from those who extended a special hand of friendship to a young, inexperienced minister.

This book offers a unique perspective made possible by long experience with the same group of people. It is based upon thousands of face-to-face visits in homes, hospitals and nursing homes. No segment of our church was more responsive to regular parish visits than those over sixty-five. In order to understand and learn from them I found that it was necessary to be with them daily. Health care specialists (physicians, nurses, psychiatrists, social workers, counselors, etc.) usually have intimate contact only when some crisis or challenge occurs. They are often denied a complete view of an older person's normal living pattern—in good time and bad, in sickness and health, in weakness and strength, in joy and sadness.

I had that wholistic experience in a very special way. Utterly unprepared, I looked upon those over sixty-five as "old" people who needed certain special services which the church could provide. I had been conditioned to see them only in terms of popular stereotypes generated by society's prejudices. Agism was not in my vocabulary. I did not know the pressures society so casually puts on its older people. My way of thinking and my limited experience precluded immediate understanding. The new congregation patiently helped me understand that those over sixty-five were just people, special only in the extent of their experience, wisdom and self-understanding. They had all the strengths and weaknesses, all the hopes and fears, and all the cares and concerns of people everywhere. I came to see them as individuals and began to minister to them according to their needs and not my presuppositions.

I had moved from a large suburban church which, while it did not have as many members, had as many people at worship and much greater financial strength. In my last year in the suburbs I had six funerals and very few people in the hospital. During the first year in my new assignment I had one hundred and twenty-three funerals and close to forty people in the hospital at any one time. In the former church I had about fifty members over sixty-five to visit; in the new parish I had over fifteen hundred. My life changed radically. I found that my training, which had seemed quite excellent, appropriate and helpful in a suburban congregation, was inadequate in this older urban congregation.

Realizing my confusion, my new parishioners spent the next few years as my teachers. They quietly corrected conspicuous mistakes and helped me understand their needs and feelings. They showed me their strengths and let me know what they could do. Most of all they accepted me, loved me, and cared about what I was trying to do.

This book is their story. It describes the exciting ministry they let me share. It is intended for three groups of people:

(1) **Seminary students** who need a realistic and helpful picture of what ministry with those over sixty-five can be.

(2) **Pastors** who need help to be more effective ministers, especially as they work with this special group of people.

(3) **Lay persons** who wish to develop a mission and a ministry among and with those over sixty-five.

I call the book **"NO GOLDEN AGERS HERE"** because one of my first discoveries was how much those over sixty-five hated to lose their individuality and how much they disliked being segregated into caretaking groups. Many of our outstanding church leaders were between sixty-five and eighty-five years of age, and they would have nothing to do with a "senior citizens group." Others of the same age were glad to participate in such programming. No one likes to be patronized. Most over sixty-five were ready to be part of the ministry—working and serving. Their golden age was no euphemism.

This book has a companion volume written for those over sixty-five who need to know how others have coped with this period of life; for those approaching sixty-five who are worried about being "old"; and for any who want to better understand those over sixty-five. The volume, **"GEE, YOU LOOK GOOD!"**, derived its title from a Red Skelton joke: "There are three stages of life: youth, middle age, and 'Gee, you look good!' " The message being that older people do look good, but in a much less superficial way than the joke implies. Many over sixty-five have learned to live and enjoy all of life, with the freedom and delight possible only for those who have claimed their own values and discovered their own identity. **"GEE, YOU LOOK GOOD!"** is for individuals who want to share that possibility.

I wish to thank those who have read the manuscript and been responsible for many improvements: Janice Hitzhusen and Leon J. Warshaw, who are very sensitive and perceptive medical doctors who specialize in geriatrics; Betty and Bob Sweet, Norman Porter, Ellis Johnson, Charles Whitford, Frank Kaiser, George Bashore and

Lois Taylor who are colleagues in mission and ministry who have been willing to share their wisdom and experience; Steve Clapp and Sue Ingels Mauck, the dynamic directors of C-4 Resources; and, most of all, to the people listed in the dedication, for they were my teachers. The long list on the dedication page represents the names of those who gave me my training. Every one of them made a significant difference in our mutual ministry. I wish the list could be ten times longer, because far more than a thousand people over sixty-five made contributions.

INTRODUCTION

When I arrived at my new church in 1967 I was full of ambivalence. The Bishop expected the church to close before 1980. Its physical plant was too large; it was in the downtown section of the city on Main Street; it had inadequate parking; its membership was much too old; it had come on bad times financially; and the city itself was regularly losing population. On the other hand, I was excited to be where there was an obvious need for ministerial service, and an important urban ministry.

Three years before my arrival, the church had professional sociologists conduct a study of its membership. A large sum of money was spent on the study which concluded that the best thing for the church was to serve its "senior citizens" in a "custodial" way, and to phase out its ministry "within twenty years." It was on the basis of this report (which was as thick as a large telephone book) that the Bishop had made his judgment.

Those were especially difficult times for American cities. President John F. Kennedy had been dead for four years; racism was evident; the public was newly aware of the poverty and neglect found in the inner city. The Viet-Nam war was accelerating and its violence was featured on the television news every night. The drug culture was exploding. For many people, the fabric of society was unravelling before their eyes. Values previously taken for granted (patriotism, respect for parents and elders, religious faith, integrity of government, the work ethic, and a common moral foundation) were under serious and widespread challenge. In addition, the picture most people had of America as an abundant land, with unlimited potential and natural resources, was being challenged. Many people became concerned about the environment, questioned nuclear energy and turned away from the "success" ethic.

In the church I had served in the suburbs, many of us had been active participants in all of the battles these issues represented. I had marched, had housed an urban black teen-ager in my home, and had helped integrate an all-white church. We had significant debates concerning the Viet-Nam war. We had worked with many young people, as they faced the temptations of the drug culture and dealt with other pressures of society.

For the first time in history a Roman Catholic Cardinal had preached at worship in the sanctuary of our Protestant church, and the community's only Jewish congregation had each Saturday used our sanctuary as its synagogue. We had built a large new church with our own hands. We thought we could tackle every issue and meet any challenge!

Then, in 1967, I was transferred to a city congregation which had almost three thousand members and constituents over sixty-five. All the problems that I thought I understood were magnified. The issues of race, war, poverty, and justice were not theoretical in the city church where few people were either affluent or powerful. Almost everyone was over sixty or under thirty. Many people did not live in a traditional family group, and the pressures I had read about became real for me. The crisis in society was far more severe than I had imagined.

I came into this ministry asking myself what I could do. I decided that the only possible avenue of ministry open to me was that of love. I would try to understand this new congregation and see what happened. For the first time in my life I confronted the question: "What does it mean to be old?" In his magnificent book, **WHY SURVIVE?**, Robert Butler defined the problem: "In truth, it is easier to manage the problem of death than the problem of living as an old person. Death is a dramatic, one-time crisis while old age is a day-by-day and year-by-year confrontation with powerful external and internal forces, a bitter-sweet coming to terms with one's own personality and one's life."[4]

I soon realized how debilitating society's stereotyping of age could be. Television taught us an ethic of obsolescence from the time we were five. The advertisements showed us what was valued (the young, the new, the beautiful, the energetic, and the fast). In every area of life (public schools, sports, business, industry, government, and, yes, even the church) everyone emphasized the importance of winning and becoming NUMBER ONE.

Many of us take years to realize how such an ethic can be both empty and destructive. Nothing is as dull and as meaningless as yesterday's winner. Former victories are forgotten because they are no longer exciting. As soon as everyone knows who the winner is, the victory loses importance. Even the powerful, the successful, and the famous are quickly forgotten when they step down and retire.

The company president, even if he or she founded and built the business, finds that most personal power is cut off immediately with retirement. Those who leave are quickly forgotten. Those who frequently return for visits become embarrassments. During their forty years of work these Americans had been taught to measure their self-worth in terms of what they could produce, and then, suddenly, without expecting it, they were out of production. In the eyes of society they became obsolete at sixty-five—arbitrarily discarded and placed apart from the mainstream of society.

America's image of old age comes as a particular shock to a believing Christian, since only one brief incident in the entire sixty-six books of the Bible pictures old age negatively. It is the Patriarchs who are the leaders, the kings, and the wise. They are the judges and the prophets. They are the priests and the law givers. Age, in the Bible, is universally respected, revered and celebrated.

Only in the thirteenth chapter of the Book of DANIEL, when two respected judges give false testimony and unjustly accuse Susanna, is an aged person presented negatively. Every other Biblical allusion to age is positive. The contrast between the view of the Bible and the view of our society is radical indeed. What is seen as a virtue in one instance is dealt with as a handicap in the other. People who have studied the Bible and absorbed its message find that its teaching is inconsistent with their secular experience and with the structure and practice of the institutional church. Age is now seen by many to be of value only in a non-technical culture where the older person can pass on wisdom. Because science and technology so rapidly bring changes, the premium in the work environment is now on adaptability and technical competence instead of experience. Almost everyone has had the experience of meeting people, including some who are over sixty-five, who are happy to have a "new young doctor." "He's up on all the latest things."

The extent of the problem is continually expanding. The society which more and more celebrates youth as a virtue and age as a handicap is rapidly growing older itself. "Agism," writes Maggie Kuhn, founder of the Grey Panthers, a political action group for those over sixty-five, "is the notion that people become inferior because they have lived a specified number of years."[5] In his extensive study on the language of agism, Frank N. Nuessel Jr. found that the language used to describe the elderly is heavily negative in scope. Here is a list of some of the words he found commonly associated with "old": "Bag, bat, battleaxe, biddy, contankerous, dodger, coot, crotchety, declining, decrepit, dirty old man, doddering, dotage, eccentric, fart, feebleminded, foggy, fool, fossil, fuddy-duddy, garrulous, geezer, Geritol generation, goat, granny, greybeard, grumpy, hag, little old lady, maid, miser, obsolete, old-fashioned, outmoded, overage, over-the-hill, peevish, rambling, second childhood, senile, dementia, senility, senior citizen, spinster, toothless, twilight age, witch, withered, wizened and wrinkled."[6]

I came into my new parish full of all the negative images of agism which I felt that those over sixty-five faced. Imagining that they had much less interest than younger people in life, sex, human events, entertainment and religion, I expected a majority to be retired in every way. I expected many to be feeble, infirm, senile, rigid in thought, old-fashioned in attitude, and conservative in lifestyle and politics. I saw them as people who needed my services. I knew that the church should minister to them but I did not see them as people who were fully alive and active in all areas of life.

In just a few months I discovered how wrong I had been. As I visited with those over sixty-five in their homes and at the church, I discovered, with quite some surprise, that they were just like any other group of people. To be sure, a few were victims of the "self-fulfilling prophesy" which society foisted upon them. They saw themselves as weak and helpless, and, as expected, they were retiring, withdrawn, and emotionally and intellectually feeble. But the vast majority were healthy, fully active, and aggressively interested in all areas of life.

They didn't want to be "ministered to"; they wanted to minister. They had a mission as valid as mine, and as varied and as interesting as any other ministry. This was just my first surprise. There was no way to safely segregate "Golden Agers" and keep them out of the mainstream of the church. They were in the center of the life of our church, both in terms of numbers and quality of ministry, whether I liked it or not. They also taught me that many churches had become institutionally closed systems, systematically pushing those over sixty-five to the outer edge of mission. In what seemed to be an irreversible process, sometimes mandated even by church policy, they were kept at arm's length, without attention given for their interests, their experience, their talents or their potential for ministry. Arbitrary rules often forced them off committees and boards and from positions of leadership because they had celebrated a particular birthday. As they lost financial clout, they often lost institutional power as well.

In the first six months on the job, after thousands of contacts, I discovered that there was not a single emotion that I had observed in young people that those over sixty-five did not experience as well. They might have had different strengths and weaknesses, but they possessed the same feelings. They, too, were joyous, anxious, fearful, excited, angry, depressed, happy, grief-stricken, neurotic, paranoid, mature, immature, energetic, lethargic, and so on. Those over sixty-five generally felt good about themselves and life for them was far better than society's images had given me to suspect.

I made a very obvious and simplistic discovery—those over sixty-five were no more a homogeneous group than any other age grouping. They too were rich, lonely, loveless, loving, working, wanted, neglected, poor, friendly, ill, healthy, antagonistic, worn out, happy, bitter, institutionalized, angry, forgotten, outcast, celebrated, and

4

fulfilled.

The Biblical view of longevity is positive partly because so few people in those days achieved old age. The response of envy, awe, and respect is modified when lông life loses its rarity. In our society, because so many more people now reach what is called old age, and because of the attitudes we have described previously, those who live beyond sixty-five often find themselves at a relative disadvantage. On the whole their health exhibits less reserve when stressed; they are more likely to be poor and isolated; and they are less likely to feel needed and wanted. Yet they can control their environment for better or for worse, as surely and as effectively as any other group of Americans. It is not a given that society must idealize youth and deprecate age. The specific and special difficulties and restrictions suffered by those over age sixty-five are different in kind, but every age group has problems. We forget how difficult youth can be and trivialize its difficulties. Do you remember how limited you thought your freedom and your opportunities to be when you were young? Can you recall how hard it was to overcome the pressures of your teen years? How seriously we took ourselves? How shy we were — confused and controlled by our peers? How bothered by superficial things (how we looked, acne, not enough money)? How pressed we were by questions of sex, alcohol, vocation, mobility, drugs, self-image, and self-respect! In fact teens and those over sixty-five have a lot in common—neither has status or a definite role to play in society.

Every age has some advantages and some disadvantages. Stripped of romanticism, youth is the most volatile of all ages. Simon de Beauvoir lists the gains and losses experienced by many people over age sixty-five. The following are usually positive gains: "pleasure in work, steadiness of rhythm, punctuality, method, close and watchful attention, willingness, discipline, prudence, patience, conscientiousness." Possible limitations might be loss of: "sight and hearing, manual strength and precision, physical resistance and suppleness, speed of rhythm, memory, imagination, adaptability, energy, drive and sociability."[7]

I found the advantages even more substantial as I visited my new parishioners and noticed that relatively few were bothered much by the limiting factors. Those over sixty-five were much more responsive to new ideas and to risk-taking than any other age group. They were willing to question any action and any value in the name of truth. As those who live closest to reality, most of them were patient with anyone who was not a phony. I discovered a pattern of behavior that surprised me. The majority of those over sixty-five supported our efforts to open up the church, to risk using the building, to serve the poor and the young, to take chances to serve the neighborhood, and to be more active in mission. Many supported the protest against the Viet-Nam war and worked hard for peace, often in confrontation with their own sons and daughters. They worked for equal opportunity for all people, especially for women and ethnic groups. I rarely found an active person over sixty-five displaying overt racism. In the life of our church they constantly supported spending our funds for work in the community, in the prisons, among the transients, in the mission field, and with our young people.

Many people approaching sixty-five are released from pressures that control their lives. They seemed much freer than their children, my contemporaries. The lay leader of our church was the son of an active couple in their eighties. I often wished that he acted as "young" as his parents acted.

Those over sixty-five had lived long enough to experience life as it is. They no longer were tempted to pretend. They were free to be honest. Most had escaped the restraints which force a person to conform. Even most of those who had not retired did not have to compromise their integrity to keep their jobs. Their values were authentic because they had worked them out:

- They had discovered how relatively unimportant possessions were. All of them had lived through the great depression when many families had literally nothing. Even so, this was often recalled as among the finest years of their lives. They had found out early that possessions were just baggage. Instead of providing happiness, possessions often brought additional worry and labor. Often they had to be cared for, repaired, insured, transported and protected. Often they caused jealousy and bitterness within the family. At a time of life when many were moving from large Victorian homes into small apartments or single rooms, decisions about possessions were often matters of heartache. Most learned that any success or value system that revolved solely around matters of wealth or possessions was empty. Possessions were often more important for their sons and daughters because they had more worldly goods at thirty than their parents had accumulated at sixty. My contemporaries were often afraid to take risks because they had to make the compromises necessary to maintain their possessions and lifestyle. They had more to lose.

- Another equally freeing discovery made by those over sixty-five involved their friends. True friends cared about you, not your possessions. Their experience had taught them that it did not pay to pretend in personal relationships. People are generally unconcerned with the victories and material success of others. Our society may shout loudly of the crucial importance of being "#1," but in a day or two the shouting stops and few care. I heard story after story about how quickly yesterday's accomplishments fade. A person works to get to the top of his or her business and then is retired. The discovery of how fast people move on without them is at first crushing, but soon that discovery is liberating. Repeated experience teaches how unimportant it is to be first in competition. The quality that is most respected and remembered is not who wins but who loves, serves, cares and understands. Those over sixty-five are free from the competitive struggle, a freedom which allows them to concentrate on life itself—on being themselves, the best persons they can be. They are free to enter into relationships with others without ulterior motives. They can love and be open without suspicion. They are free to enjoy today without worry about the possibility of future success. As the ego factors fade the happiness that comes from pure and honest choices comes clearly into focus.

• Another liberating factor for those over sixty-five is the telescoping of time. No longer is eight hours or more of each day bought and paid for by someone else. The hours of each day belong freely to each person, probably for the first time since childhood. In addition they no longer waste time on phony behavior. There is no boss to please and no necessity to live up to other people's expectations. Those over sixty-five can make the self-conscious decision to live for themselves, and, for those people for whom they love and care.

Because they were free, the spirit of those over sixty-five renewed our church and shaped our ministry. Their freedom liberated our entire church from the bondage that had contained it. They brought a commanding spirit because:

(1) Most were free to be honest. If I wanted an unvarnished opinion or some candid advice, I went to a member over the age of sixty-five. They were the best evaluators I had because they had so few vested interests.

(2) Most were free to take chances. They weren't as interested in what "others were thinking" and were a lot more interested in what was "right" and what Christ would expect of us. They also had many of the best new ideas because they were not chained by the threat of being wrong.

(3) Most were free to serve. The traditional binds of time and family pressures were not as absolute. Those over sixty-five were free to make their decisions according to who they really were. Their questions were real questions: Is the job worthwhile? Can I do it? Should I do it? Not only did those over sixty-five claim freedom for themselves but they shared that freedom with their church. Because of their powerful place in the decision-making process of the church, many of the congregation's decisions were made more honestly. We did far fewer things for show and did many more things for service.

(4) Most were free to love. Since so many of their ego needs had been quieted in the experience of living, they were able to give of themselves selflessly as no other group. In countless instances I saw them risk the act of love in the most difficult circumstances.

(5) Most were free to be themselves. Most persons over sixty-five in my new parish had taken over their own lives and no longer spent much time pretending. They didn't care about impressing me or anyone else. Instead they looked at each opportunity and challenge on the basis of human need.

(6) Most were free to be socially concerned. Many had lived through years of personal struggle in the quest of individual success. Both those who had made it and those who fell short had discovered that the quest was hollow. Many now wanted their lives to count for something beyond themselves—they wanted to wrap themselves in a cause that really was important. They were willing to be used by Jesus Christ as helpers in our community and in mission around the world.

(7) Most were free from strong ego needs. Their pleasures now came from real accomplishment not from recognition. They had already accomplished what they felt they had to do. They had seen their children through to adulthood by providing their values, and looking after their physical growth, emotional security, and intellectual education. While the results were rarely perfect, they recognized that they had done all that they could do. Most had gone through the transference of their individual ego needs to their family and children. Now they realized they would have to choose new goals.

It was this remarkable group of people—freer in almost every way than any other age group—who taught me what a church could be. This book is their story. They did not feel obsolete or "used up." They were not ready to phase out or to retire from life. Instead, they were looking for happiness and fulfillment in exactly the same way as they did when they were younger, but with a significant difference. They had a much clearer picture of where to look. They wanted SECURITY but understood the difference between the false security of possessions and the inner security of self-respect. They wanted to be LOVED AND NEEDED but distinguished between the superficial ego-recognition of temporary victory or competition and the real accomplishment of those involved in serving, caring love. They wanted some ADVENTURE in life but they had discovered that honesty and freedom are essential for meaningful life. Nothing that is faked or phony can result in real satisfaction. They wanted to identify with causes greater than themselves. They had learned that individual pleasure is seldom equal to fulfillment. They were willing to risk themselves in the service of Jesus Christ because they believed that in Christ, life found its meaning.

Many took the attitude of Nadine Stair who wrote on her eighty-fifth birthday: "If I had my life to live over I'd dare to make more mistakes next time. I'd relax. I would limber up. I would be sillier than I have been this trip. . . . I would take more chances. I would take more trips. I would climb more mountains and swim more rivers. I would eat more ice cream and less green beans. I would perhaps have more actual troubles, but I'd have fewer imaginary ones."[8]

All the difficulties of age chronicled by Simone de Beauvoir were apparent in the lives of the older members I visited. They had the health problems, the neurotic stresses, the spiritual crises, and the social pressures; however, without many exceptions, these were people who had learned how great it is to press against your own limitations. They responded to real Christianity just because it made heroic demands on them. They were at their best under extreme testing. They didn't allow the pin pricks of a thousand little annoyances, common at any age, to get in the way.

The fact that our church was dying brought them alive. The city was their home and had been home for fifty or more years. Their decision as they joined together to save their church was exciting to watch.

CHAPTER I
A NEW VIEW

Those over sixty-five were not willing to sit around and wait for the rest of us to provide services for them. I had thought of them as "Golden Agers" and immediately started a Golden Age Club to "meet their special needs." It took me more than a year to learn that I had made a mistake. Eventually they chose another name and the group and its activities took on a more service oriented form. It was never the center of participation for those over sixty-five, except in a recreational way. I learned that those over sixty-five expect the same responsibilities and the same services in their church as do people of any age. They:

- **Need to be needed.** Those over sixty-five are called to be disciples as clearly as anyone else.

- **Need the security and the challenge of a relationship with Jesus Christ.** Their lives gain meaning as they come under the saving grace of Christ and as they accept Christ as Lord and Master. Many people see clearly the need for a savior. They wish to escape the pressures of meaninglessness, death, despair, failure, and isolation. Few recognize that Christ cannot be "savior" for those who do not accept Him as Lord. Christ's act of salvation requires the response of discipleship. The two, Jesus (Savior) and Christ (Lord), go together.

- **Are a singularly vital part of the community of any church.** Bonhoeffer suggested that the Church was "Christ existing as community." Christ is head of the church and the congregation acts as His body, His agent in the world. Probably the most common mistake the church makes involves the tendency to single out those over sixty-five as a special group to be served.

No group can lay aside the call of Jesus Christ without serious loss. St. Augustine reminds us that happiness comes only to participants: "A man is not happy if he does not have what he loves; or if he loves and it is hurtful; or if he does not love what he has, even though it is perfect good. The happy life is "when that which is man's chief good is both loved and possessed.""[9]

The Christian church is that unique place where every person is valuable and needed and where every person is able to love and be loved. One seventy-three year old man said: "A few years ago I realized that I had been making a costly mistake in my life. I discovered that I still measured myself and all those around me by the standards of youth—standards of immaturity that I had long since outgrown. I recognized that that yardstick didn't fit anymore. I didn't want to be powerful, I wanted to be loved. I didn't want to be successful, I wanted to be needed. I didn't want to be a winner, I wanted to be a helper. I thought that out after I realized how much more fun it was to lose games with my grandchildren than it was to win them. I decided to be myself and accept my maturity, and I've been happy ever since."

Those over sixty-five don't have the desire to kill time the way children do. It no longer drags by; it flies. It is the most precious of their possessions and its supply is continually eroding. One person expressed it this way:

"The trouble with retirement
I'll tell you in a rhyme
Is, when you take a coffee break,
You're wasting your own time."

They need time to dream, time to play, time to work, time to imagine, time to celebrate, time to serve, and time to understand. This fact applies especially to an institution like the church which has a genius for wasting people's time, for giving them busy work.

We have killed the expectancy of many congregations by making everything we do commonplace. It was those over sixty-five who taught me how dangerously debilitating busy work is. I initially recruited them only for safe, repetitive, dull busy work without giving any thought to what such work did to them. Their honest feedback caused change in my ministry and in the life of the church. We began asking big questions before we did little jobs:

- What does the Gospel require of us?
- What needs to be done?
- What are our priorities?
- How do we spend our time?
- Does that match our priorities?
- Does this job really need to be done?

Task forces redesigned our entire mission and ministry based on what we had learned. It began with a conversation I had with a seventy-eight year old woman in my office. We were folding special bulletins for an evening service at which we were going to raise money to help an A.M.E. Church in the city to purchase a parsonage for their minister. She said: "I've been thinking how rapidly my life has slipped by. It's like snow sliding down a roof. Before you realize it has started to slide, it is suddenly crashing down. I've got to get out more. I can't stand being bottled up in myself. Can you give me something worth doing?"

As I rode home I felt ashamed. This woman wanted to get to work, to do things worth doing, but I had only seen her as a person who needed services and not as a person WHO NEEDED TO BE NEEDED.

This discovery led to a new attitude. We began to recognize the gifts of all our members. We made lists of what really needed to be accomplished and what skills every one of our people had. There was literally no limit to what was possible. Everyone in the church, however old or infirm, possessed some needed talents. We also found that few had reached their natural boundaries.

We began to see ourselves as an extended family that needed to give attention to what each member of the family could contribute to the greater good. We decided, in the light of the Gospel, to concentrate on the needs of the people around us instead of upon the survival needs of the institution. We spent no more time dreaming about a future which might never come. Instead we decided to be in mission today. The Pastor-Parish Committee Chairperson, Don Nelson, said: "Blaine, you worry too much about the future. Our job is to minister today and let the future take care of itself. If we are faithful today we have been fruitful. I don't care if this church exists twenty-five years from now. I do care if it misses the chance to serve today."

I had been overwhelmed by the pressures of a gigantic building of seventy-three rooms and a sanctuary that seated more than 2,000 people. My mind had been on survival, not ministry. I had unconsciously put institutional survival ahead of mission.

CHAPTER II
THE EXPANDED STAFF

Our first step was to take seriously a phrase then popular—the ministry of the laity. We felt that no minister should do anything that a lay person could do as well or better, and we found that there were embarrassingly few things that our laity could not do as well or better.

The decision was made to invite carefully selected lay persons who would make a specific commitment of time (from ten to sixty hours a week) to become members of the church staff. Those who made such a commitment as volunteers became regular members of the ministerial staff. The volunteers were treated in every way like the paid staff with the single exception of financial compensation. They came to all staff meetings, shared confidential discussions, carried out regular assignments, voted as equals concerning all decisions, and planned and shaped our mutual ministry. Most of the time the regular staff included six paid members and seven to nine volunteers. In addition, some forty to fifty people at any one time gave at least ten hours a week as "part-time" extended staff members. Their responsibilities were project-oriented and tended not to be ministerial in nature, but their work was no less important.

Without question our church was able to grow and be far more vital in mission because of their arrangement. I believe that the Bishop's prediction that the church would be closed by 1980 would have been prophetic without the new ministry provided primarily by those over sixty-five. Instead the church is much stronger today than it was then and thousands of people have been helped and challenged.

Obviously a great majority of the staff volunteers were people who were technically "retired." All had skills and abilities equal to paid staff members. All were under the same committee supervision as were paid staff members.

Those that worked twenty or more hours a week as volunteers had various responsibilities:

- ordained ministry
- business manager
- building superintendent
- supervisor of ministerial visitation
- supervisor of hospital visitation
- supervisor of home visitation
- parish co-ordinator

Only two of these people were under sixty-five. Many others worked less than twenty hours a week. At no time was a majority of the paid staff under sixty-five, and our decisions were made democratically. A majority of those on the volunteer committees which shaped policy for our church were also over sixty-five. However, young people were warmly welcomed and included in all the most influential positions of the church. As many, if not more, women than men were active in positions of power. The young people came to be in the majority on most committees before the end of the thirteen years due to the sensitivity and planning of those over sixty-five.

Few people realize before they arrive at old age how young a person can feel even at a very "old" chronological age. Leo Tolstoy wrote in his **LAST DIARIES:** "I remember very vividly that I am conscious of myself in exactly the same way now, at 81, as I was conscious of myself, as 'I' at five or six years of age. Consciousness is immoveable. Due to this alone there is a movement which we call 'time.' If time moves on, then there must be something that stands still, the consciousness of my 'I' stands still."[10]

Although few of us see ourselves, especially in our inner selves, as "old," it is hard to come to terms with the shortening span ahead. Eric Erikson wrote that "Although aware of the relativity of all the various life styles which have given meaning to human striving, the possessor of integrity is ready to defend the dignity of his own life style against all physical and economic threats, for he knows that an individual life is the accidental coincidence of but one life cycle with but one cycle of history, and that for him all human integrity stands or falls with the one style of integrity of which he partakes."[11] It was this integrity that filled our staff meetings with insight and wisdom.

Selecting volunteer staff members was not very complicated. Invariably people had already shown excellence and dedicated service in the various areas of need. If they had been outstanding it was a simple process to visit with them and ask if they would be able to take on a major responsibility and an expanded time commitment. A few had good reasons why they could not accept, but many gave positive responses immediately. Some who could not make a major time commitment became very active in our wider lay ministry program. The personal qualities we looked for were:

- a deep and contagious faith in Christ
- a self-giving happy personality
- a disciplined commitment to follow through on accepted responsibilities.

Our "full-time" volunteers performed the following variety of ministries:

- **Ordained Ministry**

Some churches have retired ordained ministers or lay pastors in their constituency. These individuals have the experience, the skill, and the maturity in faith that every church desperately needs. Roland Sundberg had retired early from a series of successful pastorates to return "home" to New England. He accepted my invitation to become a full ministerial member of the staff as a volunteer, and did everything asked of him, covering every ministerial function immaginable. We usually had four other full-time paid ministers during the thirteen year period, and Roland's ministry was as effective as any of those four. He preached frequently, made hospital and home visitations, taught adult and youth classes, cared for many special projects, and often volunteered to do difficult jobs that none of us wanted to do. Roland was a valued counselor and an exceptional and talented musician. I note three things about his contribution:

(1) **He was most relaxed and unthreatened.** Since he was a volunteer he was not looking for advancement or salary increases, nor was he bothered by criticism. His freedom from external considerations and pressures gave me a new appreciation for "Quaker-type" volunteer ministries. His witness was given a unique integrity and authority because he was a volunteer as well as a fully ordained and experienced pastor.

(2) **He was free to follow his convictions** and didn't have to modify his witness in any way. We were benefited because his values were Biblical, his preaching challenging, and his example impressive.

(3) **He was an enabling minister** who extended his ministry in many ways by involving, recruiting, and training others. He multiplied his witness many times by not trying to carry it alone.

Dr. Leslie H. Johnson, who had been a District Superintendent, came on staff full time a few years before his retirement. After he turned sixty-five, he became a part-time staff member but often worked a full week. A capable, strong organizer and administrator, Les had the ability to keep things together. He organized services for those who were shut-in and directed our extensive ministry to older adults with special needs. He was especially good in recruitment and counseling. Les had sufficient self-confidence to allow those over sixty-five to be in charge of their own programs and groups, and helped them to share in every aspect of our common ministry. He developed creative recreational and educational programs for our seniors and was active with many other groups.

- **Building Superintendent**

George Richardson, our building superintendent, was an especially remarkable person because his influence extended to every part of the parish—including devotional and spiritual life. His spiritual depth enhanced our staff meetings and, to me, his spiritual counsel was at least as valuable as the thousands of hours of physical work he volunteered. As a retired engineer he had the technical background necessary, and as a former executive he had the management skill and organizational ability we needed. He supervised the day-to-day work of our custodians and the many volunteer repair and maintenance groups. His commitment, like the others, was for twenty hours a week, but often he worked forty, fifty and sixty hours a week when there were special projects or emergencies. The church went through several major renovation and repair projects under his direction. He also was very active in the music ministry, and involved with every special show and production. In prayer groups and in mission projects he was always among the leaders. I am convinced that the freedom a volunteer possesses makes accomplishments possible that no paid person, however capable, could accomplish. Although there can be jealousy, that too, is a learning experience, and tends to be less prevalent among volunteers than among the paid staff.

- **Business Manager**

Roger Palmgren was the person who brought our church the same skills and professional ability that he had previously given to the business world. He was "retired" when he joined the staff, but he was as hard a worker as I have ever observed. He was usually at the church by 7:30 AM every morning, and often was still present late in the evening. His title, Business Manager, did not adequately describe his activity level. He reorganized our entire operation, brought us through a period of terrifying inflation, dramatically increased our financial strength, and did all this, while energetically supporting greatly increased giving for service projects and missions. Roger always was willing to take a chance and able enough to make what seemed impossible happen. (He cut our oil consumption fifty percent a year and, at the height of national inflation, raised enough money so we could send a new missionary to Africa.) He also fought to allow the building to be used by the young people. He supported its use by teen-agers and children and welcomed the poor and oppressed from the neighborhood, fully realizing the extra cost in maintenance.

- **Director of Home Visitation**

Rosalie Benson worked as a nurse for thirty-six years and then joined our volunteer staff as supervisor of home visitation. She recruited dozens of people to visit others, let each of them know they were loved, needed and understood. She arranged thousands of small services of love: birthday cards and parties, home care, doctor's visits, appliance repair, voter registration, food shopping, an ear examination, a luncheon "to get her out of the house," and so forth. She brought a compassionate concern for everyone in need into our staff meetings. It was her genius to carry a contagious spirit of love with her wherever she went. Her example encouraged many others to serve in a similar way. We later developed a telephone contact on a daily basis with every shut-in, ill, or troubled person in the parish. Most of the volunteers were over sixty-five.

- **Director of Hospital Visitation**

Ernest Lucas organized lay hospital visitation. For several years he planned a daily visitation schedule so no one hospitalized would be forgotten. Not limiting himself to members or constituents, he sought out, through an elaborate system, all those in our seven hospitals who had no regular visitors or any church home. He made thousands of visits himself and brought many new people into the church. Both he and Rosalie provided the pastors with a communication tool that was priceless: they made us aware of where the need was greatest.

The next two positions were filled by volunteer staff members much younger than sixty-five, but those persons involved many people over sixty-five in the carrying out of their work. These two exceptionally talented women brought the skills of professionals to their assignments. We mention them because in another church these positions might well be filled by persons over sixty-five.

- **Supervisor of Ministerial Visitation**

Marilyn Bateman, who for a decade, as a volunteer, ran an exceptional senior high youth program, joined the staff with the difficult assignment of director of ministerial visitation. Our large staff of ministers needed coordination so they could avoid duplication, so more visits would be made, so people would not be forgotten, so the visits would be timely when the need was greatest, and so the parish might continue to grow by seeking out new members. Marilyn accomplished a complex job with diplomatic skill. Much more service was accomplished because she cared enough to push. I know that I made more home visits each week because I had to report in to Marilyn every Thursday morning. If Monday night came and I had accomplished only ten or twelve visits, on Tuesday and Wednesday I concentrated on visitation. I was amazed at how much more productive I became with an accountability structure. I would have said that I was visiting "as much as I could" if I had been asked before this program started. It is certain that the church benefited from a large increase in ministerial home visitation because of this program.

• Parish Coordinator

Velma Tattersall as parish coordinator was perhaps the most effective of all our workers. She arranged every social event, coordinated all celebrations, planned effective church usage, and directed most of our major special projects. She also had a genius for problem-solving by using a task force. She was especially valuable to our staff because she was always pushing us to be less parochial. Her interests extended far beyond the walls of the church. She got involved in community, district, conference, state, national, and world concerns. Wherever there was a need, Velma put things together to meet that need. Hundreds of people were helped because Velma made that need known and gathered people together to meet it. As an additional responsibility Velma organized a remarkably productive flower ministry. Every Sunday eight to twelve (sometimes sixty to eighty at Easter or Christmas) bouquets of flowers were delivered personally to members in hospitals or nursing homes by a team of volunteers that Velma recruited. I was often thanked for services that Velma's group performed.

These people not only gave a minimum of twenty hours a week in volunteer services (in fact much more) but they and all the other lay volunteers paid all of their expenses. Thousands of dollars were given in service through automobile expense, food, gifts of kindness, record-keeping and even building supplies and office materials. I would estimate that less than ten percent of all direct expenses supporting volunteer services were ever paid by the church. We just couldn't afford it at the beginning, and by the time we could, people had taken their second mile giving for granted.

Recognition also should be given to the paid people on the staff who worked well beyond their sixty-fifth birthday. Ruth Berrett, the executive secretary of the church, was sixty-three when I arrived. She continued to work full time until she was seventy-six. Few persons occupy a position for fifty years! In many ways she was the first of the volunteers because she worked, literally, seven days a week, three hundred and sixty-five days a year. For more than a year during the depression she worked full time even though the church could not meet her salary. As the center of everything we did, she was the flywheel who kept the vital statistics and the needs of 3500 and more people in her head. She often worked ten and twelve hour days. She radiated the qualities of honesty and freedom. We all knew that the church and its mission were Ruth's first and greatest love, so she could give honest advice and criticism that never would have been accepted from someone else. If you wanted the truth all you had to do was ask Ruth—and often you would get more truth than you wanted, sometimes without asking! She patiently supervised more than twenty office volunteers. Out of financial necessity we dropped our office staff to one paid. The fact that we were forced to turn to so many volunteers proved a blessing. Each week we published an eight page church newspaper and a bulletin, cared for hundreds of pieces of mail, and handled many special projects in the church office.

Ruth was always open to new ideas. When there was a great controversy involving the use of the church facilities for basketball, Ruth, who had to put up with the interruptions, noise and confusion, energetically supported the new activity. At the high point of a bitter Administrative Board debate she said: "It's about time we had some life around here!" I believe that her enthusiastic support of people fifty or sixty years younger than herself opened the doors of our church and, in many ways, saved it.

It was natural for Farnham Goulding to work for the church after he retired, for he had spent forty years as a volunteer in every facet of its life: working with youth, the church school, the United Methodist Men, the Men's Bible Class, the trustees; in finance, in stewardship, in mission, and in outreach. He joined our staff as a parish visitor and as Director of Stewardship.

Farnham gave thousands of hours, often helped by his brother Paul, to the "little tasks of love" so desperately needed and greatly appreciated by people in trouble. He got a hot meal, went to the laundry, brought false teeth to be repaired, saw that an electric razor was sharpened, hired boys to mow the lawn or shovel the driveway. In short, he enabled hundreds of older people to live more securely and comfortably in a climate of Christian love.

Esther Salme worked with amazing effectiveness for the church, first on the paid staff and then as a dedicated volunteer, parish visitor, and evangelist. For many years she was an aggressive and effective advocate for those who were retired. A wonderful source of creativity and innovation, Esther began many new programs. She was a magical visitor, able to bring joy into every situation. She fought for those over sixty-five, insisting that both the church and society grant them social services commensurate with both dignity and need. She kept an elaborate record over many years so that we knew at a glance who was not present at morning worship. She would make dozens of telephone calls each week to people not present to let them know that they were missed and to find out if they were sick, or needed any services we or others might provide. She made countless follow-up visits and even saved lives. One Sunday morning she missed an older man who was always at worship. Since he didn't have a phone, she called the landlady of his apartment house. He was found prostrate on the floor of his living room. Since he had suffered a stroke, his doctor said that "he might have died" if Esther had not missed him. She cared for everyone on a personal basis, and saw to it that everyone had at least one friend. In the thousands of hours she worked as a volunteer her ministry was as valid and as productive as that of any ordained minister.

Esther was a "Doctor of Involvement." She made every person feel needed and gave everyone something important and "wonderful" to do. She was the finest "motivator" I have ever seen. Esther enabled hundreds to capture the excitement and adventure of Christian living, witness, and discipleship. She communicated so effectively because she lives such a happy, loving life herself. Her answer to the question: "How do you get someone who has not been convinced before they reach age sixty-five to begin living a life of caring, serving love?" was simple and traditional. She spoke of conversion, of turning a person from a life of selfishness to a life which shares in the love and salvation of Jesus Christ. Hers was a ministry of challenge. She refused to allow a person to settle for less than the best that God intended. I heard many times of Esther inspiring a depressed person to become interested in life again.

These were the full-time volunteers, but the real story is that of the 1,000 other people over sixty-five who were involved in ministry and mission. The only thing any of us did was to let them know how much they were needed and how fulfilling life could be for them if they spent their time giving loving, caring services to those around them.

Often it has been the psychology, even of fine churches and good ministers, to treat their older members as if they were precious alabaster jars of perfume. They were given custodial care and carefully segregated. It was as if the church were afraid of risking them in the real world and intent on protecting and shielding them from life.

Those over sixty-five in our parish refused to accept the role we would have given to them. Their experience, their talents, their wisdom, their example, and their caring services proved to be crucial. They were ready to pour out their lives for Christ, finding meaning in their lives through their ability to minister to others.

Our church came alive because they lived out the vision of Isaiah: "he giveth power to the faint; and to them that have no might he increaseth strength. Even the youths shall faint, and be weary, and the young men shall utterly fail; but they that wait upon the Lord shall renew their strength; they shall mount up with wings as eagles, they shall run and not be weary; and they shall walk, and not faint." (Isaiah 40:29-31 KJV)

If you think your church is filled with people over sixty-five who are just passive "Golden Agers," hoping to quietly withdraw from society, you just don't know them well enough. Visit with them. Listen and find out how they feel and what they need. You will find that they need the same essentials you do:

- to be loved
- to be taken seriously as persons
- to be listened to and accepted for what they are
- to be active doing interesting things
- to be really needed by at least one other person
- to be occupied with concerns other than self
- to be responsive in faith to the Lord Jesus Christ

CHAPTER III
CHRIST EXISTING AS COMMUNITY

The church is the "Body of Christ" (1 Corinthians 12) where "varieties of gifts" (Romans 12) are shared. The church at its best is an extension of Christ in ministry. With this perspective in mind I will describe the ministry provided by those over sixty-five within that local church community and their mission to the wider community and the world. Then I will share the suggestions and services they provided for their peers over sixty-five who needed special help and outline, briefly, a theological foundation for this ministry.

Those over sixty-five made an essential contribution to every facet of our ministry. They were active in the generation of ideas; they were generous with their time and talents; they were the teachers and the scholars who pushed the rest of us back to the Bible and out into the world; they treated concerns of mission seriously and most gave themselves to mission without reservation; they were the cement which held our Christian education program together; they gave exceptional support to our youth programs and our college, business and service groups; they organized and carried out stewardship drives and kept our financial affairs in order; and they were the foundation for our evangelism and visitation programs—the spark and the example for the rest of us! As exceptional listeners and counselors they improved communication within the church family. They helped many individuals through times of personal crisis. They gave loving care to church property and support to the fine arts. I expected to find them resistive to change and instead found them the leading supporters of new forms of worship, devotion, Bible study and prayer. Here are a few of their contributions in these areas:

- **Worship and Devotion**

The finest gift any church can give its people is a positive experience of worship and devotion. Like the rest of us, people over sixty-five see the rhythms of worship in the light of their own experience. Their lives alternate between periods of strength and weakness. They have walked long in life. Their sores have been rubbed and their doubts tested. Their witness of faith has authenticity and power not found in new converts. We are told that the dominating feature of contemporary life is that of change at an ever-accelerating rate. Worship can be a constant that allows an ade-

22

quate response to change. There are five types of change—all of which impact on the way we worship:

(1) **Changes of style including mores, morals, values and ideals.** Worship and devotion provide an environment in which one can distinguish between the significant and the trivial. The word "worship" derives from the old Anglo-Saxon word "worth-ship," meaning the recognition of worth. Psychologists have concluded that communication is more effective when the truth is positively stated. Those over sixty-five viewed worship as the time when Christian mores, morals and ideals would be lifted up before God. They respected an attitude of openness and mutual discovery, but they preferred to concentrate on essentials.

(2) **Changes in science and technology.** In the past sixty years our lives have been fundamentally changed by science and technology. None of the major forces in the community are as they were sixty years ago. In 1925 the radio was new and television still in the process of scientific development. There were no rockets or satellites. The movies were just beginning to talk; Lindberg was yet to fly the Atlantic; there was no commercial aviation and the automobile was to be the province of the rich for a few more years. Worship on Sunday morning, Sunday evening, and midweek was, by far, the leading continuous communication and entertainment event of American society. The preacher was a combination of the television commentator and the movie star. It was the age of the pulpiteer! Now the Sunday evening service is past history in most of the country. It was unable to compete with television shows produced at a cost of a million dollars an hour. On Sunday morning, television and radio preachers encourage millions to stay at home.

Scientific and technological change has also been influential in changing the content of preaching. In 1925 there were no sermons on the atomic bomb, on thermonuclear war, on environmental issues, on energy crisis and conservation, or on the mobile society. Bible study alone set the worship emphasis for most, without pressures from any other media. Since then the media has flooded homes with issues that only the most conscientious preacher mentioned in 1925: racism and injustice; liberation of the economically and politically oppressed; the starving and the hungry; sexism and the lack of justice for women; poverty and urban decay; prison reform and capital punishment, and so forth. Technological and scientific change has transformed the content of sermons. Those over sixty-five spend more time than others responding to media (watching television, listening to the radio, reading newspapers and magazines and books) and thus they tend to be among the best informed members of any congregation. They insist on relevance. They want their worship experience to underline and relate to that which they have addressed dring the week. I regularly received more feedback concerning sermons and worship from this age group than from any other.

(3) Change in our perspectives and attitudes. We are now all citizens of the world if not the universe. Many boundaries that were taken for granted and used to contain us have been quietly and gently broken:

(a) Boundaries of dialect, accent and language. Television has brought us all to one way of speaking, or at least to one way of hearing. Soon computer research will give us instantaneous verbal translation of language through a voice synthesizer.

(b) Boundaries of information. Many of us now see the same television shows and the same movies. Cable television has had great impact.

(c) Boundaries of competing churches, faiths and philosophies. In our ecumenical society people know much more about the beliefs of their neighbors and, perhaps, much less about their own religious heritage. They are far less likely to be blindly arrogant, judgmental or intolerant.

(d) Boundaries of credibility. In past times the minister was often the best educated person in the community. This is almost never true today. Thus, laity will not be as likely to quietly accept all content in the sermons offered to them, and they will have much more content to offer themselves.

(e) Boundaries of age. Since everyone has access to the same media, age differences, especially in ideas and spirit, are less wide than ever before. A case can be made for a separate youth culture (from 12 to 25), but those between 26 and 85 are more likely to be tuned into the same news and the same concerns. Their different life experiences shape much of their response to those issues and concerns.

(4) Change in the tools of decision making and problem solving. In 1925 Edison, the solitary genius, was still the model for inventors and problem solving. Now a world of computers and digital equipment has reshaped the way people think. "Systems analysis" and "operations research" have taught people how to handle an incredible number of variables simultaneously, continually testing various ways of meeting defined goals. As the new thinking process continues to accelerate, our practice of worship, especially its dependence upon one preacher as the vehicle of truth, may have to be reexamined. Various sources of input, including that of laity of all ages, can make worship more creative and communication clearer. The church should be using different and more varied voices in the forming of its community.

(5) Change in personal freedom and in variety of individuals' alternatives. We now live in a highly mobile society where people have thousands of options open to them. **The church is no longer the center of life for most people.** It has become one option in direct competition with all the other worthy causes seeking time, talents, and personal support. This change is especially important for churches who have many people over sixty-five in their membership. In 1925 those few who lived beyond sixty-five just continued working. Only a few homes had radios, and none had television. Churches had little competition from social, community or entertainment events. Older members of our church continually reminded me that the church has to be more than another club to sustain their loyalty. In fact we usually can't do as much for their health, welfare, and entertainment as can other community services and groups. Worship was of crucial importance, for it centered on the meaning of life.

These changes affect profoundly every activity of the church. The church which emphasizes those functions also provided by many other groups (social, ethical, legal, political, recreational, educational, and service) is bound to see its importance in the lives of its members shrinking. Those churches which emphasize that which is unique to them—worship, devotion, Bible study, mission, ethics, and morals—are likely to play a much more important role in both the lives of their members and in society. That does not mean that the church should move away from the functions that duplicate or add to services provided elsewhere, for the church does have a vital social witness, but it does mean that the effective church concentrates on its essential function.

Those over sixty-five have been affected by these changes in special ways. The rapidity of change may cause them to think that they are receding from an increasingly complex world. They may feel apart—not needed by anyone or useful in such a society. They are retired, often from a work experience that was the center of their interest and, perhaps, no longer even exists. They are ignored by most advertising because they are no longer primary consumers in the economic market. To the extent they are good parents they will let their children live their own lives. They are continually losing friends and relatives. **One of the few institutions in America that desperately needs those over sixty-five is the Christian church.** For both quality and quantity the church must have the experienced ones in its fellowship. Contrary to the thinking of some church growth experts, to be effective a church must be heterogeneous. Homogeneous churches may grow more rapidly but they do so at the risk of being less than a church. **Older people have insights, skills, experiences and values without which no church can live.**

Many people over sixty-five perceive life in much the same way as lonely newcomers to New York City do. They can see thousands of people every day, yet they know few by name. The church can be the great exception. Christ always saw people in terms of their potential. He knew who they might become, what they might accomplish. The church inherits this revelation. Worship can be a channel of Christ's power of new birth and transformation. Its gospel proclaims that it is never too late for deliverance. Especially for the old and the infirm the church can be a "rock of refuge" and "a place of peace." It can be the agent of protection and is called to be the place of deliverance and salvation (Psalm 59). The church is the place in the world where people are free to fail, since the Christian hope is not for any personal victory or corporate success. "This is the only place in which I feel I belong," one woman stated. "I'm not wanted anywhere else. I'm not needed anywhere else. I'm not understood anywhere else."

Paul said to Archippus: "see that you fulfill the ministry which you have received in the Lord" (Colossians 4:17). That charge defines the mission of the church, a mission that concentrates on those in need. Worship is the central experience in the life of the church, because it is the event that witnesses to the "why" of life. Like the theme of a great symphony, worship develops rhythms of its own:
- praise and acceptance
- confession and forgiveness
- thanksgiving and celebration
- prayer and supplication
- revelation and challenge
- witness and service

Worship underlines the essentials of life and certifies its meaning and value. Its inescapable by-products involve commitment to Christ and a Christian vocation for every person. Worship can be that time of revelation when we realize not only how much Christ has done for us, but also what Christ can do with and through us. At any time of life, the discovery that we belong to Christ, that He loves us, and that He has a purpose for our lives, is overwhelming. **The word of the Gospel makes clear that a person's value does not in any way depend on his or her current condition, or on anything they have said or done.** In fact, our preoccupation with our own performance, our own successes, inhibits our real self. Often we are so full of self that Christ cannot speak through us. Nevertheless, God accepts us as we are—at any age or station in life.

The good news is that we are loved and that we are needed, and, even more, that we are called to be agents of that love. Plato said: "The eyes of the spirit begin to grow sharp when those of the body begin to fail."

If individuals are denied, even for a short period, participation in worship, that ritual of life which celebrates faith and love, they lose touch with the source of their security and their meaning as persons. This is why worship is so crucial for those over sixty-five. In a culture which doesn't want to do anything more than once, which is always ready to choose anything new and faddish, which is too busy for reflection and too noisy for contemplation, worship is often the only possible path to fulfillment. At the very least, it is a time of confession and forgiveness. Everyone wants to belong somewhere in the world, to have some status, some sense of importance. Confession is the act of understanding one's place in the world. It is the antedote for the competitive conditioning of our society, an alternative to the success-ethic which pressures one to become "Number One." In the quietness of worship a person can discover that Christ's standards of judgment are not like the standards of the world. He does not certify our goodness on the basis of our position, our power, our knowledge, our wealth, or even our age. As we confess in worship our hidden fears and doubts, our sores and weaknesses, and our pride and our vulnerability, we begin to understand why and where we belong. To accept the forgiveness of Christ is fundamental at any age. The knowledge that we are accepted gives us all the status we shall ever need, status before God. Such forgiveness frees us from all competitive striving to be better than others. The Gospel reveals that we are needed to share in His ministry and that we belong and are forgiven because of the work of Christ.

Many people over sixty-five told me that they found for the first time in worship that they could accept themselves, that they belonged, and that they were needed. The sacrament of Holy Communion was most often the means of forgiveness in our congregation. It was offered every week and a high percentage of those people who communed weekly were over sixty-five. They told me:

- "The Lord's Supper gives me the only power I need. It allows me to accept myself and to offer myself for renewal."
- "The Sacrament is my power for the road. It charges me every week. He helps me to forget my own pain and concentrate on helping others."
- "Communion with God gives me what strength I have and what I hope to share."

George Santayana wrote: "Nothing is inherently and invincibly young except spirit. And Spirit can enter a human being perhaps better in the quiet of old age and dwell there more undisturbed than in the turmoil of adventure."[12]

This judgment proved to be true in our congregation. Among the most thankful were those who had experienced the most pain. **I was initially amazed to find that the happiest parishioners, the most willing to celebrate, were frequently those in the most difficult financial circumstances, or those in the poorest health, or those under the most pressing demands.** Often the people fighting poverty or those sick with cancer adopted the rhythm of thanksgiving and celebration while those who were much more comfortable in life were frustrated and anxious. A very ill woman of eighty-two wrote me: "You know that I am usually happy and thankful about my life and my son, who has done so well financially and has good health but is so anxious and critical about life. I think it is because he is under so much pressure. He is always being tested, always under somebody's gaze. I know who I am and I've accepted myself. I am thankful for all that I've seen and for what I still can do. I wish I could help my son see that it is who you are and not how much you do that is critical."

Many of those who lived and worshipped with this spirit of thanksgiving found their blessings in the little things of life. They may have once hoped for the great or the extraordinary, but they had lived long enough to understand that such aspirations were often unrelated to their real desires and not essential to happiness and fulfillment: "It took me sixty years to find out what made me happy. I wasted so much time chasing the irrelevant and the trivial." One man wrote: "I think I have never been as thankful as I am now. Old age has taught me the importance of timing. You get too much in life before you know what to do with it. I can assimilate my blessings better now because they come a little slower and are less anticipated."

Worship is so important to those over sixty-five that it may be that the most important single service they need from the church is an adequate transportation plan that provides dependable service to and from each worship opportunity.

A corporate discipline of prayer, both in public worship, in small groups and within the family means as much as any other form of worship. In prayer each of us can lift our words of adoration and praise, offer our thanksgiving, confess our weaknesses and our failures, and ask for forgiveness and help in the future. On March 1, 1788, when he was eighty-five years of age, John Wesley wrote in his Journal: "I considered what difference I find by an increase in years. I find (1) less activity; I walk slower, particularly up hill; (2) My memory is not so quick; (3) I cannot read so well by candle-light. But I bless God that all my other powers of body and mind remain just as they were."[13]

The attitude of thanksgiving can be a fleeting moment of recognition soon to be put to one side by the pains and troubles of life. To sustain such a spirit one needs to express thanksgiving regularly in prayer. One man said to me: "Prayer keeps me from being downed in the flow of a week. I am not always very satisfied with my life. Prayer helps me get things in order."

Prayer was the greatest single source of strength for my older parishioners. In both private devotion and corporate worship, prayer can be either rewarding or dangerous. It can concentrate attention on the self, emphasizing need and ego satisfactions, or it can focus thought on Christ and His mission in the world. One can choose a "give-me" attitude of prayer or a "use-me" attitude of prayer. Early in his life St. Augustine prayed: "O God, make me pure, but not now."[14]

We found that a sense of humor helped in prayer. A good way to start a period of meditation is to count how many times we needed to laugh at ourselves during that day. Without intending to, all of us can be pompous, foolish, bitter, selfish, arrogant, stupid, petty, and supercilious. Such actions trace our need for forgiveness. When we get a true perspective on ourselves, we are ready to pray. Prayer is an "opening up" process in which we have the chance to discover ourselves and our values. When we allow God to enter our consciousness, and if we are receptive, then a never-ending process of constructive change and fulfillment has begun.

In corporate worship, prayers of intercession allow us to concentrate on the worshipping community and the needs of people around the world. Several people over sixty-five developed prayer lists which were regularly circulated throughout the parish. We found it helpful to pray for others by name. Every person in our congregation could be assured that several others were praying for him or her daily.

The best preaching I heard during my years at that church was done by lay people, young and old. The most unforgettable person I found in the church was a retired black man who may have been "old" chronologically but was as vital and as intense in spirit as a person could be. He taught one of our high school classes for twenty years. Each of my four children reported that he was an outstanding teacher. A magnanimous person, he kept barely under control the anger and moral outrage that was part of his soul. A black man who came to maturity just before World War II, his life represented the story of the great forces that came to collision in mid-century America.

The great force in his life was his mother. I never met her but she was a legend in our parish. Forceful, honest, loving and demanding, she set standards that are influential even after fifty years. Many people told stories of her radiant personality and her sacrificial service. She seemed to influence every person with whom she came in contact. She had fashioned her children in her image.

I shall not forget Spencer telling a high school youth group of his experiences during World War II. He had tried to volunteer, but was rejected because he was black. Later he was drafted and forced into a segregated food-service unit. He felt no identity with such values and hoped America might wake up to what it was doing to its own people. After the war he worked in a succession of laboring jobs, which allowed him time to give his leadership to the church and the community. He possessed the rarest qualities—wisdom, dignity, and faith. No one could be in his presence without feeling the force of his character or the presence of his moral witness. Spencer preached in various ways—at worship, in board meetings, in church school classes, in small groups, and through the example of his life.

Spencer was magnificent, but the church had many people who were able to enrich our worship through their preaching. Their contributions in worship meant a great deal to our church. In my imagination I came to the city in a burst of self-sacrifice, thinking that they needed me. Instead I found myself being spiritually fed by the congregation. Here was a church with a living faith to share. Their long heritage of exceptional ministers had shaped a congregation of Biblically informed disciples. Perry Howe was one of many lay preachers and theologians serving in the church when I arrived. At the age of eighty-eight, he had helped to mold the values of a generation. Even the young people listened to him eagerly. I loved to attend the church school class of seventy-six-year-old Clover Knowlton, for she consistently found things in the Bible that I had missed. Elsie

Kenworthy, a seventy-five-year-old woman from Scotland, wrote books on obscure Biblical passages and could make any one of them come alive. Equal in power, and more interesting than any seminary professor of my experience, she gave one hour lectures every Sunday morning to a large class—and was an excellent preacher. Helen Erickson, seventy-two, knew with precision each part of Scripture and insisted on applying it to every social problem. She would gladly rub our noses in the Biblical ethic until they were raw, yet she was neither judgmental nor somber. She taught with humor and wit. Marion Rossland, who had lost her husband to cancer, supported every social cause that demanded loving service, including the most controversial.

Harry Hedenberg lived full-time in the service of others and possessed the common denominator that our best disciples possessed, sparkling eyes and a warm smile. His personal dedication was so effective that people listened with care when he spoke. Ed Dahl, a retired pastor, could put more in a benediction than many of us could pack in a twenty minute sermon. I wish there were space to chronicle a dozen more who preached with their words and their lives. Our worship was enriched by the witness of those who lived according to the Biblical word. **They were patriarchs and matriarchs gathered at the center of our lives. They still had the power and the charisma of prophets. For the next decade they added to our spiritual and devotional life.** As of old, they provided the birthrights and were the judges who made the crucial decisions. They acted out the prophecy of Joel: "Hear this ye old men . . . Hath this been in your days, or even in the days of your fathers? Tell ye your children of it, and let your children tell their children and their children another generation" (Joel 1:2-3).

Not one of them was judgmental in attitude or spirit. When they preached they spoke of the sufferings and the tragedies of life, not only with words of comfort, but with words of inspiration. They did not dwell on a heavenly faith but pushed us back into the world with spiritual strength. They were people who were secure enough in their Biblical foundations to ride above the sorrows and disappointments of life. They saw the Christian life as a calling, and refused to release anyone, especially their contemporaries, from responsibility and service. I admit that I sometimes listened to them with shame. **These "older" people, who I had thought would be "puttering" around were utilizing all their talents to change lives around them, including my own.** They asked not for possessions, or honor, but for work to do. Like the Psalmist (27:14): "They waited on the Lord: Be of good courage, and He shall strengthen thine heart."

These people were strong because they were really needed—they lived in a community, formed by Christ, where no one was wasted or obsolete. They lived according to the Biblical injunction: "Bear ye one another's burdens. We then that are strong ought to bear the infirmities of the weak." (Romans 15:1) As one woman said: "A nice thing about being old is that you can't hide your needs. Since there is no possibility of faking indifference, it isn't so embarrassing for people to help."

The basic rhythm of life—fulfilling human need with loving caring service—is the word of God for individuals. It is the acting out of Christian pastoral care. So many people are like Bob Hartley on the "Bob Newhart Show" on television. In one episode he got a new beeper and it never beeped! No one ever needed him or wanted to talk to him. Since most of our membership lived in the city, there was no shortage of human need in our community. Ours was a church where the beeper was always on! It was obvious that all of us were urgently needed if our ministry was going to get done.

Sometimes we did not realize our own strength or think in a large enough frame of reference. Too often churches don't risk enough to be effective. In fifteen years we watched, while dozens of churches in our downtown area closed their doors. Almost all of them played it safe. Even though they had much larger endowments, they tried to cut back on activities in order to survive. We might have been hyperactive, but we were involved in the lives of people, advancing rather than retreating. We tried:

- **to risk our strength on program rather than on building.** While others were cutting back we moved from one and one-half ministers to four full-time paid pastors plus the voluntary staff.

- **we evangelized.** Thanks to Ed Mason and his teams of visitors we found people where people were not supposed to be—all types of people—those that lived in a city, the young and the old, as well as families from the suburbs.

- **we got involved at every level of the community:** the prison, the jail, model cities, schools, human rights concerns, all service groups. Today a woman from that church is mayor of the city.

- **Pastoral Care and Those Over Sixty-Five**

During the first few months I was in the city parish, some twenty-five people graciously held teas in their homes so I could meet twenty to twenty-five new parishioners at one time. In this way I was able to make many initial, if superficial, contacts and listen to a good many statements about the state of the parish and its needs.

My colleagues had prepared lists of those who had various difficul-

32

ties of health, depression, family crisis, and bereavement. It was soon obvious that our ministers could not give personal attention to the number of people who needed care. Most of them happened to be over sixty-five years of age. During the same period I met a large number of people, again mostly over sixty-five, who had unusual sensitivity and great personal ability. Many of them had backgrounds in teaching, the social services, or nursing, and all had successfully moved through periods of crisis themselves. They were healthy and full of energy. It was obvious that they could give needed counsel to older adults. Many had both the time and the interest.

In our efforts to give pastoral care the ministerial staff made no pretense to be what they were not—medical doctors, psychiatrists or psychologists. Our plan was to refer parishioners to a professional after three or four visits unless the problem was primarily of a spiritual or theological nature. Unfortunately a great majority of our parishioners could not afford private counselors and all publically supported counseling centers had long waiting lists. They were unable to schedule an initial appointment within five or six months. Family service case-loads numbered well over forty which made certain that personal contact would be minimal even after counseling could be scheduled.

We therefore faced a dilemma. The need was great and by itself our staff could not begin to meet it. Since the ministry of our church was so visible in the community, active in the prison, in the hospitals and in the neighborhoods, many more than our large membership depended on us. Also, during the first year, the city dropped its traveler's aid service. Since we were the only church to list the pastor's home numbers in the telephone book yellow pages, many stranded transients came to depend on us.

We asked our retired members to help, first those who had been professionals themselves—doctors, school teachers, social workers, and lawyers—and then those who had been through similar crises themselves. This proved to be a most valid extension of ministry. The program was never publicly announced to avoid spotlighting the helpers or those persons needing help. Those asked to participate were carefully screened and were all given training and orientation. They were advised to be themselves in every circumstance, empathetically sharing care and love. They reported regularly, and quickly referred any problem or unusual situation. The program was informal and there was no therapy or treatment offered. **We were friends who cared, who had time to listen and were ready to love.**

The program started slowly but eventually involved thirty-three people who had regular contact with several hundred people over the years. They concentrated on four types of referrals:

- Those in which the counselor had successfully gone through a similar experience.
- The person needing help was lonely and depressed.
- A person was in a period of bereavement and grief.
- A person had an economic or an employment problem.

The results were often remarkable. The volunteer counselors had tremendous advantages over the full-time ministers and other trained professionals:

- They had sufficient time. They could meet with people as often as needed.
- They could visit with them in their homes.
- It was not a job for them. They were present because they loved and cared.
- They were people with affirming, radiant personalities who had remarkable compassion and acceptance.
- Many had been down the road themselves and had sensitivity and respect for the difficulties and the pressures faced by the other person.
- They shared the faith and the values of the person needing help.

Although our sample was much too small for statistical purposes, I noticed that in comparison to the more than one hundred people whom I referred to professional counselors a much higher percentage of the more than three hundred people that the lay counselors worked with were obviously and substantially improved. Several later became helpers themselves. Only four or five times was the effort obviously a failure and, in each case, I was clearly at fault because the match had been poorly made.

It is my conviction that our society underestimates how important a supportive family environment is for mental health. Few people are strong enough to overcome by themselves the real pressures of poverty, isolation, the death of a loved one, and personal failure. I also believe that the importance of love and a strong faith is not adequately recognized. For a healthy life everyone needs contact every day with at least one loving friend.

One of the few wealthy parishioners I have had belonged to my first student parish. She was a millionaire, lived in a mansion, had several servants, owned a bank and one or two businesses. She lived alone with a full-time paid companion-secretary. I had known her for a year as a most active church member when she requested a "favor": "I want you to call me Agnes. No one else in the whole world calls me by my first name." From that time on, even though she was fifty years older than I, I called her Agnes. I have often thought of her in the years since her death. She had every opportunity and every possession a person could want, but she lacked the most important support in the world—someone who cared enough to form an honest relationship with her and who could love her without the possibility of an ulterior motive.

In a sense, pastoral care in the extended family of the church was an attempt to provide every person with at least one friend. Those over sixty-five did this job for me in a remarkable way. William Schofield, in a well-known study, has statistically demonstrated that psychotherapists tend to treat the young, the attractive, the well educated, and the successful (which means well-paying). "The American Psychoanalytic Association study reported by David Hamburg and others showed that 98 percent of psychoanalytic patients are white, 82 percent are under 45 and 78 percent are college-educated. In contrast, only 6 percent of the people over sixty-five are college graduates and one-seventh are functionally illiterate."[15]

One may feel that professional help is best, but in a large and growing city parish this was an ideal, since the vast majority were neither affluent nor predisposed to such care.

We noticed that a great many people over sixty-five experienced a predictable incongruence in their lives. There was a discrepancy between their self-image buttressed for years by the standards of society (the importance of possessions, of position, vocational success, etc. in defining self) and their actual experience in old age. Often they were unaware of the incongruence and fell into a pattern of symptoms that could be diagnosed as forms of mental illness. We found that if a loving, caring, accepting counselor spent time with them, giving them unconditional positive regard, they became able in that environment of love to accept themselves again. Many were able to build a new and positive self-image.

More than two centuries ago John Wesley wrote: "Dear Sister Beemis: When you write to me, you have only to 'think aloud,' just to open the window in your breast. When we love one another, there is no need of either disguise or reserve. I love you, and I verily believe you love me; so you have only to write just what you feel."[16]

Such an approach to a parishioner may seem simplistic by today's standards but we had abundant evidence that such an approach still is effective. The counselor took on his or her own person the pain of the other, giving love in support. The ways of God are mysterious. Often ministers and professional counselors come from a different world, with a distinct vocabulary. They know too many solutions, quotations and methods, words that mean very little to the person in need. Such a person might express thanks, but later remark to a friend: "You know he (or she) meant well, but didn't really listen." (I have been taught this lesson a great many times, for many people have walked past my door to make contact with a lay counselor who may not have had clinical training, but who did share the gift of a caring and listening love.)

Many older people discover that personal qualities which were once considered assets have suddenly turned into liabilities. The mother who has given all her love to her children now sees that same love looked upon as possessiveness and intrusion. The father who prided himself in being a constant companion for his children and a strong provider sees the efforts that once drew cheers now sometimes bring annoyance and damaged pride. Sexual urges that were looked upon as both natural and rewarding are now viewed, often by one's own children, as somehow repulsive and absurd. A person's love of family, home and heritage, once viewed as the hallmark of the upstanding citizen, now becomes viewed by some as sentimental nostalgia or an "unhealthy" clinging to the past. Every older person can furnish additional examples of the transformation of valuable attributes into serious problems.

Another older person who has been through such disconcerting experiences is often in a much better position than a professional to offer a sympathetic ear and to help sort out the real from the imaginary, the important from the irrelevant. The work of the counselor is something like that of a detective who looks for clues, feelings and motives as well as "facts." The best detectives are able to sharpen their analysis of the situation because of their own experiences. The older person as counselor knows and understands why the other person is suddenly crying, can't sleep, and finds the present so threatening. Often the counselor has experienced a similar environment, similar pressures, similar pains, and similar problems. That can be a tremendous advantage.

Every person is at one time or another overwhelmed by life, and everyone collects a few resentments. The bitterness, anger, and confusion which are sometimes part of old age can best be understood by one who has faced the same pressure. Negative attitudes are rarely chosen consciously. They can often be changed by the positive input of another person who understands and cares.

The "counseling" or "friendship" role was extremely valuable for the helpers themselves. Their accomplishments were obviously so important that they received great satisfaction from them. Only one or two did not ask for another assignment, and every one spoke of their delight in sharing the ministry of pastoral care. (A negative should be mentioned: as word spreads concerning the helpers, some people will volunteer for pastoral care who are not ideally suited for such ministry.)

• Youth Work and Christian Education

In many churches children and teen-agers are carefully segregated from those who are over sixty-five. It is thought that they "inhabit" different worlds and consequently can't accommodate one another. Our experience was much to the contrary. In the same way that teenagers and grandparents have excellent personal relationships, so integrated contacts of young and old in the wider family of the church are usually beneficial to all concerned. In church school we found a natural affinity between younger and older people.

In one of my student churches the nursery class had been taught by the same woman for three decades. Her class was the most important event of each week for her. It gave her a specific purpose. That which brought to her life a positive self-identity, itself was wonderful fun. Children would talk about their experiences in her class for years. I thought at the time that she was a dramatic exception. I now believe that her dedication is typical of the spirit, the care and the ability older adults bring to any church school.

Many older teachers have more time to give to preparation and planning than do younger teachers. They also have the time and patience to follow through during the week. One teacher increased the attendance of her class by making telephone contact with each child each week. Others called each absent student to see if they were ill and to encourage regular attendance.

The grandfather or grandmother image is often the most comfortable and positive for the children. Often the affectionate hand that those over sixty-five hold out to children is more easily grasped than a parental hand, particularly on the junior and senior high school level. One of our college students wrote a letter to her sixth grade church school teacher: "My first thought as I arrived at college was of you. This would never have happened without you and your love. Entering your class in the sixth grade is, so far, the most important event of my life. You enabled me to believe in myself and to find a meaning in my life."

One Sunday morning I entered a classroom a few minutes after the class was finished. The teacher, a woman of sixty-eight was on her hands and knees, carefully collecting the beads from a broken necklace. A small girl was watching her with sorrow. In about ten minutes the teacher was able to fix the necklace and the girl left the room beaming. The teacher turned to me with a smile: "Before I got started teaching here my life was like that broken necklace. I felt as if my life was broken. My emotions were spilling all over the place, and nothing was holding me together. You don't know how much this class means to me. It keeps me alive."

When a teacher is excited about his or her class, teaching is a grand experience. The mix of old and young worked even better in the high school and college years. For many years, Howard Brewer conducted a class for those out of high school, a College-Business-Service group. It covered all the books of the Bible and all areas of life, shaping a way of life for three generations of students. Much more than a class, it became the center of social and recreational life, a counseling center where care and understanding were available, a "dating service," a place of vocational decision and commitment, and a place where lifetime values and morals were constructed. Howard kept a personal relationship with his students as long as he lived, with annual reunions and many home visits and letters. Many people told of the difference this man, who taught through his seventies, made in their lives.

One of our best teachers taught until he was eighty-six. A public high school teacher and a Biblical scholar, he taught without any notes. A master of his subject, he was so vitally involved with it, that the magic of his class was enough. He made no attempt to be involved with the students outside of the classroom, but he was so interesting, as well as a bit eccentric, that his attendance average was the best in the church school. His humor was powerful on several different levels. His scholarship, including his knowledge of the original languages, was profound.

There was a large adult church school with a clear majority of the students and many of the teachers over sixty-five. Rarely were there less than a hundred adults in attendance, and it was the central event of the week for many of them. The contrast in the teaching methods of our various teachers was interesting. The variety included:

• A class taught by an aggressive Scotswoman who loved controversy. Her class was an exciting turmoil, dominated by her sharp thrusts and sense of drama. Hers was the lecture method, followed by questions, challenges, and not a few battles.

• There was a men's class, with close to fifty involved (the great majority over sixty-five) with a different man teaching the lesson each week. A President and a Secretary organized the assignments and the projects. Following a democratic process, they could choose any topic, but most frequently they were studying the Bible.

38

• A cooperative class led by three women who were all over seventy. They liked to change lesson topics. The average unit rarely lasted more than a few weeks and then the class moved on to other areas of concentration. Its members gained a good deal of mutual support from one another in times of difficulty. It traced a continuous existence for over sixty years. (It is worth noting that older adults are better able to make the commitment of regular attendance to a seven or eight week unit than they are to a year-round, permanent class. When you share a beginning every eight weeks, you feel free to come and do not feel left out.)

• One class specifically concentrated on social and ethical issues. Its leader brought every political and moral topic under the spotlight of the Biblical word. The fallout from its discussions often made our board and committee meetings more interesting.

• There were also discussion classes and a lecture class where one could just sit without any risk of unwanted responsibility or pressure.

For many years those over sixty-five were the backbone of our church school. In the beginning they were essential to its survival. By the end of the period they had passed a healthy church school on to a new generation while many remained as students to learn from a new generation of teachers.

Older adults were constantly involved with our active youth fellowship groups. The teenagers were directed with remarkable zest and creativity by young couples, but there was continuous interaction with those over sixty-five. Many seniors helped as counselors on trips, retreats and special events. Two men came on every retreat as our chefs. They prepared the meals and became beloved friends and counselors for the teenagers. They taught by their example of love in the finest way possible, influencing many lives by their listening friendship, by their caring and by the giving of themselves. Many young people told me that Arthur and Spencer were the first true adult friends they ever had. Each year the youth group celebrated the two men's contribution with a party in grateful thanksgiving for their unique service.

Another senior was our expert on "media." He even purchased a third motion picture projector himself so no movie would have to be "unprofessionally" interrupted. Sid developed many visual aids for our program and always helped provide transportation.

Over the years the youth group took special trips to many parts of America and to foreign countries—to visit missionaries, to learn about another culture, and to have fun. We went to Japan, Spain,

Portugal, England, Scandinavia, Mexico, and many places in Canada and the United States, including Alaska and Hawaii. Those over sixty-five were very involved in every aspect of these trips—planning them, raising the money to make them possible, as counselors on the trips themselves, and as teachers who brought appreciation of new cultures and historical background. Since almost all the youth were city youngsters, who never before had the opportunity to go on a major trip, these trips were extremely important in their development. For many it would be the one foreign trip of their lives. It is no exaggeration to say that the support of those over sixty-five made the youth trips possible. Travel brought many exciting adventures as several generations shared a magnificent common experience.

We carefully selected those who worked with youth. It was almost impossible to make a mistake because those older adults who were willing to work regularly with youth fit in so well. (In our case, a mismatch was so rare as to be unique.) Those who had the energy, interest, faith and self-giving love to come forward to tackle such a regular and difficult assignment were always people who brought grace, patience, honesty and joy to the task. When our young people had to deal with the pressures of the sixties and seventies—drugs, someone over sixty-five cared, listened and loved. Many young people were helped in fundamental ways, breaking a destructive habit of correcting a major mistake, without their parents ever knowing, allowing the young people to maintain more positive family relationships.

One teenager confessed that he was a "drug-pusher." He had "turned-on" five girls and two boys in our group. Immediately three "seniors" whom I trusted began to work daily, over several months, with these young people. All of the youth were able to conquer their drug habits. The parents of two of the girls never even realized that their daughters had been brought through a problem. On another occasion one of our young people had to be transported to a drug rehabilitation center in Kentucky. A man of seventy-two made the trip, both to deliver and later to pick up the young man, and I doubt if anyone in our church ever knew the purpose of his "vacation."

We often had guest speakers do the program at our senior high youth group. At least a third of these people were over sixty-five. Because their life-shaping events (the depression, World War II, Hitler, the baby boom, atomic energy, cybernetics) and the resultant morality ("making-it" and striving to be #1) were so interesting to to-day's youth, they were natural choices as speakers. Discussion with them seemed to come easier and more naturally to our youth than did communication with their parents or with those of us who belonged to their parent's generation. They were not threatened

40

because those over sixty-five seemed to understand and emphathize with their point of view. We were able to explore issues of racism, exploitation, drugs, patriotism, war, sex, welfare, atomic energy, oppression, and poverty far more effectively with our intergenerational model.

The old and the young also joined to present several musical and theatrical programs involving many people. They sustained an active sports program. The youth contributed their energy and competitiveness while those over sixty-five had the enthusiasm of fans.

Intergenerational cooperation was also used to conduct service projects. We published a booklet listing all scholarship opportunities: local, county, city, state, and national, covering church, governmental, and private grants. We held a common Christmas party for teenagers and senior citizens, as well as a common New Year's Eve party. Several people over sixty-five formed an ongoing correspondence with young people as they went away to college or entered the service. No group did as much to build effective youth work and Christian education in our parish as did those over sixty-five.

• Work in Finance

As you might expect, since both our Business Manager, Executive Secretary, and Building Superintendent were all over sixty-five, this area was substantially influenced by senior citizens. A majority of the Trustees, the Finance Committee, the work area on Stewardship, the Property and Usage Committee, the Parsonage Committee, the Budget Committee, and the Special Gifts Committee were usually over sixty-five. No area of church work was accomplished as effectively and as well, and no area was less dependent on clergy support or involvement. They were not often conservative. The building was to be used and risked. Again and again when challenges were made to prevent building usage by youth or for community events, it was our older group who had the free and adventurous attitude that prevailed. When others were content to give up, they were ready to press on.

The Trustees, under the direction of Win Russell, Stanley Barker, and Harry Spencer Jr., spent many months trying to plan housing for senior citizens, laboring over community zoning problems, and expanding our program. Much of the repair and construction on the church buildings was accomplished by dedicated volunteers, most over sixty-five. Almost every portion of our large church (73 rooms and a sanctuary seating 2200, a basketball court and bowling alleys) was repaired in those years, including a new roof, new windows, repainting and sand-blasting all the exterior stone, much interior construction and repair, a new heating system, a new parking area, a major renovation of the organ, a number of new offices, and new landscaping. Over the same period, at least as much money was raised to send beyond the parish to help others as was spent for ourselves. When we celebrated the structure's fiftieth anniversary, the church taped a living history—recording the memories of those who had worked the entire fifty years in the new building. It recorded how the building was erected and paid for during the great depression—what an accomplishment! Church workers, as well as many others in those days, often missed paychecks. There were times when many people thought that our church would not survive.

Win Russell, the Chairperson of the Trustees, grew up in the church and it became his great love. Over many years, he gave an amazing amount of time, talent, and peacemaking ability. His greatest value was his spirit of good-will and caring love. He was always full of good humor, warmth, and support. On the most difficult of issues, amid great controversy, he was a consistent and heart-warming supporter of all that was good. He was involved in mission. We went together to the police station in the middle of the night to help three children gain release. We bailed water for hours after a flood. I remember his ability to fix anything. Most of all, I remember his remarkable smile when we were under pressure or in trouble. Those were days when confrontation over social concerns was inevitable, and there were occasionally spiteful, even vicious attacks. Even when he disagreed on the issue, he defended the right of witness and the freedom of the pulpit. Like many other parishioners over sixty-five, he was quick to defend his pastor, even when he thought him wrong.

During the same period many of my ministerial peers were preaching the same message and taking the same positions on the war in Viet-Nam, racism, and oppression. I believe that I was saved from much angry denunciation because of the love and the compassion of our post sixty-five leadership. They knew that love and approval were two different words. Never once, in contrast to the experience of many of my colleagues serving other churches, was I threatened with economic or political pressure. Never once was I under attack from some without strong, caring, loving support from others.

- **Visitation and Evangelism**

The bulk of the visitation program was accomplished by people over sixty-five. Our program consisted of three levels: (1) Finding new members; (2) serving our current membership and reclaiming those who had become inactive; and (3) crisis emergency visitation, including hospital and nursing home visits.

(1) Finding New People: In order to reach those who lived in private homes and in "three-deckers" we used a weekly publication, BANKER AND TRADESMAN, which listed each change of property in our area each week. It was more difficult to reach those living in apartments or rooming houses. We were forced to use telephone books, street lists and personal contacts with people already in the rooming house or apartment complex. Our program involved at least four contacts with each new person:

(a) A survey call made by one or two lay persons within two weeks of our first receiving the information. The visitor brought a warm welcome and took a religious census. If the family had a church home we thanked them for their cooperation. If not, we asked seven questions to obtain an overview: size of the family group, age of children, previous religious affiliation, any current family needs, the length of time since their last move, the type of church they were looking for, and if they would like us to notify any other denomination of their presence in the community. Our visitor left a pamphlet telling the story of our church, a photo, and a map showing its location and the various parking lots.

(b) One of our associate ministers, usually Ed Mason, made a follow-up visit to those identified as possible new members. This visit was occasionally made by laypersons who were on our volunteer staff.

(c) Following the new person's first time at worship, the preacher of the morning would make a visit within a week.

(d) The two lay persons would make a welcoming visit to begin a process of assimilation into the service and work opportunities offered by our church.

A great majority of the lay visitors were over sixty-five. For the first few years we tried to match the age of the visitor with the age of the prospective member, but this proved to be an artificial division. An older visitor could often make a young family feel at home and tell the story of the church's mission better than anyone else. I remember their extraordinary dedication. One man reported: "I haven't climbed stairs for years and now I'm going up stairs every day for you." Another called his wife every half hour to be sure she was all right because he didn't like to leave her alone. I kidded him about "the nice, short visits he had to make." Two retired school teachers always visited together, and often found themselves making surprise contacts with their former students. One man, who had no children, built up such a close relationship with a young family he visited that he considered them his surrogate family. Often the patient sensitivity of our older visitors drew out personal needs and extended the caring ministry of our parish.

(2) **Serving our currrent membership and reclaiming those who had become inactive:** Since a great majority of those who needed in-home visitation on a regular basis were over sixty-five themselves, it was natural to turn to their peers to expand the ministry. They formed an extensive network which made hundreds of visits each year. Each shut-in or ill person was visited at least once a month and many were visited in their homes each week. The ministerial staff was promptly informed of any emergency, any change in condition or feeling, or any special occasion. I had the habit of celebrating the birthdays of parishioners over eighty. Despite my inability to carry a tune, I have sung "Happy Birthday" to a great many people over eighty. With one woman I celebrated each birthday from her eighty-third to her ninety-eighth year. Her health always permitted us to eat at a public restaurant. Since she had no family, the waitresses joined in the singing.

One visitor wrote on a report: "I am so excited about the new friends I have made. I had forgotten my own potential. I found that I could do much more than I thought I could, and I am glad for the push."

Rosalie Benson organized the visitations and made good use of the special skills our members had. Our visitors did many errands, much shopping, some repair work, and often made several extra visits, when the need was great. Sometimes the monthly contact took on a daily responsibility during emergencies.

Velma Tattersall organized special events of celebration for people over sixty-five. Her wonderful parties brightened the lives of a great many people. She also organized extensive services at both nursing homes and hospitals.

(3) **Crisis and emergency visitation—including hospital and nursing home visits:** Our pastors visited hospital patients at least three times a week. Ernest Lucas organized lay visitors so that most hospitalized people had contact with the church each day.

Hospital visitors need special training if they are to be effective. Often hospital visitors act like embarrassed strangers—people with whom patients have to become reacquainted. This poses an unwanted energy drain on patients and involves emotional strain that they do not need. The same spirit of sympathy which is often appropriate in the home of a lonely person now seems like pity. The good humor so effective elsewhere can now appear to be blustering and unnatural heartiness. In addition, most people are tempted to describe how they or a close friend had gone through an "even more difficult time of hospitalization." I found that three training sessions could greatly improve the effectiveness of visitors. Here are my current recommendations for such a program:

(1) At the first session invite six or seven articulate people who have recently completed a period in the hospital as patients (at least four days). You will be surprised at the varied advice they will give. Ask them to go through their day as a patient, speaking of needs, concerns, or experiences that helped and experiences that hindered. Give them two books and ask that they be read by the next meeting:

> Norman Cousins: *Anatomy of an Illness*
> Morton T. Kelsey: *Healing and Christianity*

(2) At the second meeting invite two doctors and two nurses from the church or a neighboring church. Ask them to discuss:
- Hospital Etiquette
- Do's and Don'ts with patients
- Give any suggestions they wish

You will again be surprised at how much the advice and suggestions vary. Spend at least thirty minutes discussing the books.

(3) Have them visit with experienced hospital visitors from the parish. Have the visitors emphasize:
- keeping the pastors and church informed. Please call for help whenever necessary.
- the importance of caring listening.
- the importance of honest humor, avoiding the pretense of cheerful heartiness.
- the importance of shared faith, Scripture and prayer.
- that we all depend not on our own wisdom and abilities, but on God's grace.

Those over sixty-five proved to be our best hospital visitors. They brought common experience and understanding, and they were often old friends who could act naturally because they had recently, and perhaps frequently, shared the same surroundings. The visitors were trained to listen and encouraged to share the quiet as well as the pain. They realized how important physical contact can be and were willing to patiently hold another's hand without speaking.

Their laughter was apt to be more genuine and self-deprecating, aimed away from the patient. We found it important not to insist on efficiency in visitation. Those that take their task seriously need time. To go in and out in a few minutes is mandated by serious illness or by intensive care units, but as patients recuperate or have to face lingering and more serious health problems, they need time. Speed might produce more visits, but it is equally likely to result in missed opportunities. The truly helpful visitor takes the time necessary to build an ongoing relationship which will eventually move beyond the present moment and provide strength when the patient returns home.

Death occurs primarily in hospitals in our society. Families and loved ones often need as much care as do patients. Sometimes our visitors were able to improve the communication between family members and occasionally served as catalysts who brought estranged people together. One man had not visited his mother who had been hospitalized for over three months. Finally our visitor sought him out at his home, and helped with reconciliation. Our best visitors shared four qualities:

(1) **They were outgoing, optimistic people of faith.** They were secure themselves and willing to suppress their own needs in order to better serve others.

(2) **They were good listeners.** Their first interest was to sense the needs of the patient and be responsive to them. They enjoyed serving people and were ready to display empathy.

(3) **They concentrated on the feelings of the patient,** avoiding current events, controversial topics, and any form of judgmentalism.

(4) **They were prepared to share their spiritual strength,** but not willing to force their witness on another. Frequently they would share a portion of Scripture and a personal prayer, but they were trained to be responsive to the situation.

(5) **In addition they were willing to do errands** and perform services for the patient or the patient's family.

Nursing homes are often the out-patient department of hospitals —where people are sent when families and doctors do not know what to do with them. These patients are often more depressed, more overwhelmed by their situation, and more neglected than hospital patients. They are certainly more lonely. Such patients need more attention and regular loving care. Those over sixty-five understand this need and are often able to bring the desperately needed contact with the outside world. Because they share similar values and are likely to enjoy similar experiences, visitors of the same age group are invaluable.

Thanks to our Minister of Music, LeRoy Hanson, who was able to appreciate and build the talent of those over sixty-five in creative ways, our church was able to bring worship services and other musical programs to several nursing homes on a regular basis. Velma Tattersall, the Church Coordinator, organized many different craft experiences and teaching units for nursing home residents, and other visitors planned day-trips and other "outside" experiences for the patients so that their confinement would not be as oppressive.

Unfortunately many family squabbles center on the nursing home experience. Such care is expensive and does drain financial resources. There were times when a brother and a sister were locked in bitter strife over the assets of the parent, often in argument concerning the cost of the care being provided. In the eye of the storm the patient had what could be horrible emotional pressure added to physical and financial strain. Our older visitors were very helpful as peacemakers in the midst of these family wars. They were often more successful than any of our ministers in solving problems and helping people over their difficulties.

• Mission and Ministry

When I first came to the urban church, I was guilty of misjudging the willingness of those over sixty-five to enter into world mission, into ministry in the immediate neighborhood and into the world of social and moral concerns. I found, to my surprise, that many were already involved and others were open to involvement. I inherited a twenty-five year heritage of support for foreign missions. Over the years our older members were enthusiastic in their support for missionaries (especially medical, agricultural and educational ministries). Those over sixty-five led the campaigns and enabled regular contact with our missionaries, exchanging letters, sending supplies and medicine, collecting clothes, and every staple known. We were eventually involved in a direct supply line to Africa which carried every conceivable product, from jeeps to aspirin tablets hidden in cotton gauze. Missionary giving for most of our members did not come out of their affluence but from extra work and sacrifice. The church took pride in giving more than its share of connectional and missionary obligations. In addition the missionary study and work of the various women's, men's, couples and youth groups added substantially to the parish total. In the most difficult of times we never sent less than $40,000 beyond our local church in a year.

Compassion for others came a bit easier to people who had been vulnerable, lonely, struggling and weak themselves. They wished to share with others in foreign lands, for they realized that, as difficult as things sometimes were in the United States, life was easier here than in most other countries.

Several of our older members became experts on missions and taught us through their contributions to the church newspaper, at board and work area meetings, and at worship. We were told that in Africa and Asia the odds were four to one that a child would not receive any medical attention at birth or at any other time in life. If the child did survive to school age, the odds were two to one against that young person receiving any schooling. For the half that entered school, three out of four did not complete elementary school, and only one in ten completed high school. The present life span for all but the elite in the third-world countries was below forty-two years of age. Our people who were over sixty-five were especially impressed by how few people reach "retirement" age in other countries. In India 3.6% of the people are sixty-five or over, in Brazil 2.45%, in Togoland 1.46%. This contrasts to about 11% in the United States and more than 12% in France and England.[17]

If the support of our older members could be counted on for foreign missions, it was even more positive for helping in our own neighborhood where they could see the problems for themselves. Those over sixty-five consistently voted at board meetings to spend our funds on community projects. They backed their votes with their gifts and their service.

A very active ministry in the county prison, initiated by and centered at our church, involved more than fifty of our members. Thanks to their persistence, the jail, the largest in central Massachusetts, was transformed, adding a high school diploma program, a trade and craft curriculum, an outmate program (including custodians at our church), counseling programs both for prisoners in jail and after their release, visitation, worship services at the jail, recreational, and job-referral programs. Thanks to Pastor Ed Mason, the program involved a great many of our older members. They helped in every part of the jail ministry, from attending the regular weekly worship and visitation programs, to getting dozens of jobs for released and furloughed prisoners.

Soon our church had a Spanish-speaking pastor, Chris Rodriquez. We helped to purchase a van for a special mission for the Hispanics in the city, and worked to develop social and spiritual services for the fastest growing minority in our area. We helped found the city's

Human Rights Commission, the first one in the country to have sub-poena powers. We were active in improving conditions at the city hospitals and in developing a "live-in" nurse program. Some members worked with a half-way house for those who had been released following problems with drugs, and others worked at the Mustard Seed, an organization working to feed and clothe the poor. Some worked at the program for alcoholic rehabilitation at Doctor's Hospital. For over two years, until public funds again became available, we were a one-church "Traveler's Aid Society." Through the Pastor's Discretionary Fund, hundreds of people were helped with food, shelter, and clothing. Often we purchased the gas that allowed them to finish their journey. As the only church listing the pastor's home phone number in the yellow pages, we answered many calls for aid. We were extensively involved in volunteer work at the State Mental Hospital whose director was an active member of our parish. The hospital, within walking distance of the church, depended on more than twenty-five of our volunteers.

At three local hospitals, our members organized and directed volunteers. Many of our senior citizens were involved. They operated the hospital gift shops and many service projects. We made a self-conscious effort to encourage our people to volunteer outside the church organization so we could serve a wider community. Our several members who were physically handicapped themselves recruited others to work with them to support their community action groups. Others were involved in working for housing for the elderly. At one time a majority of the members of the housing authority belonged to our congregation. Many worked for the Salvation Army, The Boy and Girl Scouts, the Y.M.C.A., the Y.W.C.A., and the Boys' Club and Girls' Club.

In a project that was initiated and completely carried out by lay people, our parish raised many thousands of dollars for materials and built with their own labor two multi-purpose worship facilities at non-sectarian Boy Scout and Girl Scout Camps. The funds were raised through a series of musicals, staged and performed by our members with more than a hundred people involved. The actual construction of the two facilities took more than two years. With other workers, more than fifty people over sixty-five worked hard on both the projects to raise the money and on the actual construction.

In Jaffrey, New Hampshire, the village where she wrote her famous book, **MY ANTONIA**, Willa Cather had inscribed on her tombstone: "That is happiness: to be dissolved into something complete and great."

That was the secret of those over sixty-five in our parish. They got involved in the basic rhythm of life. They were needed for they gave loving, caring service to others. There are dozens of other examples that could be given. You will find that there is more than enough worthwhile work to do in your community, if you are willing to take risks—if you challenge those who have the time and the ability to serve.

Equally significant were the steps many of our older members took on their own to serve their community. Several accepted into their homes young people who had difficulty with drugs or had been juvenile delinquents. One senior citizen, whose husband had worked forty years for one company and had no pension or death benefits at all, led in changing the state law to protect people from similiar treatment. A black lawyer continued to practice after retirement. He represented hundreds of poor clients, often receiving no compensation at all. A black social worker used his retirement years as a volunteer counselor for those involved in university and urban confrontations. I heard the chairperson of the board of one of our universities give him credit "for a fair settlement of the grievances of the black students" on that campus. Both these men were in church worshipping every week, but they did not have the time to be active in our institutional structure for they were busy acting out their Christian witness elsewhere. Some churches fail to realize that the most important place any of us can carry out our Christian discipleship is in the world.

I was proud of the work our members did to sustain community neighborhoods. Many people wanted to tear down our Central Y.M.C.A., which was located in a depressed area of the city. They wanted to rebuild it in a safer, suburban location "where it would be much easier to raise funds." Both the volunteer chairperson and the full-time executive administrator were active church members (on our church Board of Trustees). They led the fight to keep the Y.M.C.A. downtown because most of the youngsters who needed recreational outlets lived there. Because of their success, thousands benefited.

Two other members, both well over seventy, were active and powerful members of the Salvation Army Board of Directors. They donated a great deal of time and talent in the service of those burdened by poverty. It was inspiring to see many people so involved in discipleship. We were often not successful in what we tried to accomplish, and a few times we made serious mistakes, but we had a sense of doing that which was ethically important. The grace and dignity which those over sixty-five brought to community action was an example for the rest of us.

CHAPTER IV
POLITICAL AND
CULTURAL CONCERNS

There is a story about a Chinese Mandarin who insisted on sitting for his portrait looking out a window which provided a view of a river and a mountain which he loved. He sat with his back to the artist and insisted that the primary attention be given to the landscape. He felt the result would give a better clue than his face to his true self.

The choices each of us make concerning life style, the environment, and values, establish our identity with far more precision than our appearance. Few people escape the injustices, the inhumanities, and the prejudices of the society in which they live. The seven freedoms possessed by those over sixty-five years of age as listed in the introduction enable them to be responsive to a ministry of social action. Questions of world peace, racism, agism, medical care, and nuclear war received the support of a significant minority of our congregation. A much greater percentage of those over sixty-five were personally involved in community action and social concerns than any other age group. Although less than a majority, those over sixty-five who did take the risk found their lives more exciting, more purposeful, and much more fulfilling. I noticed how much those involved seemed to enjoy each day and how they felt vitally drawn to worthwhile accomplishments.

In a sense they had moved beyond their personal battles with selfishness, and they were beginning to take responsibility for the world they inherited and helped to shape. Often they had personally accepted Jesus Christ as Lord and had been led into an attitude of caring concern by means of the Gospel. Through outreach and social engagement they found out that self-fulfillment did not depend on security, but in personal commitment to a cause bigger than themselves. Unlike Linus from the comic strip PEANUTS, they did not need a security blanket, but they needed challenging opportunities.

We made a significant time commitment to many of the major political and cultural issues of that time. We believed, because of the systemic nature and incredible complexity of many of societies' problems, that corporate political action alone could result in basic changes of those societal factors which cause injustice:

(1) **Economic Injustice:** There is real value in corporate fact-finding concerning economic realities, poverty and unfair employ-

ment practices as a result of racism, sexism, and agism. Finding the facts of economic distribution and human need and clearly stating them was an important task. Often people who took part in fact-finding endeavors registered surprise and were much more open to change once they discovered the facts themselves.

(2) Delivery of Human Services (especially public safety, fire protection and family services): Our programs in these areas, including programs against crime and vandalism, in cooperation with the police, is described in detail in the companion book, **GEE YOU LOOK GOOD!** These programs were successful in the most dangerous parts of the city.

(3) Legal and Counseling Services (including Spanish for Spanish-speaking prisoners): We provided these services for many persons who were in jail or in trouble with the law.

(4) Canvassing State and Federal Commissions: This survey work assured that those over sixty-five would know the great amount of public assistance available to them through state, local, and federal government sources. Volunteers sought the facts and made them available to others.

• Self-Discovery

Many of us suspected that there were injustices suffered by those living in the worst areas of the city in contrast with those who lived only a few miles away in suburbia. Fact-finding was successful because it led to a change in policy by several local businesses and by agencies of city government. From many interviews and questionnaires we discovered:

• The same supermarket chain charged from 15 to 27% more for the same item in the inner-city stores than it did in suburban branches. At all locations, packaging was for families. Single portions, needed by single and retired people, were either unavailable or only available at a higher price. The chain changed both policies after a period of negotiation and publicity.

• Those food items which underwent the most rapid inflation were those most likely to be purchased by the poor, while those items purchased by the affluent went up much less dramatically. The study was done three different times over fourteen years, and the results were consistent. We tracked a hundred items for an eight month period. Products which demonstrated the greatest amount of inflation were: powdered milk, peanut butter, cereals, cheaper cuts of meat (including hamburger), cake mixes, canned fruit and juice, tuna fish, canned mackerel, soft drinks, and staples. The products showing much less inflation were: spices, lobster, the best cuts of beef, fresh fruits and vegetables, table wine and frozen food.

We were unable to effect any change in this pattern because we found that national chain policies were not affected by local complaints. Many products are priced because of national advertising campaigns (or lack of same) and are set at central headquarters.

• We conducted fact-finding projects in all sorts of areas: the time that it took firefighters to respond to alarms in various sections of the city; the consistency with which the building and health codes were enforced; the treatment of tenants in poorer neighborhoods; the policies of local movie theaters (we learned that all nine movie theaters were programmed from the same outside source; no local manager had control over what was shown; thus few films of interest to those over sixty-five were shown.); the attitude of police with regard to young offenders; the attitude of employers concerning ex-convicts; job market opportunities for teen-agers; the type of religious programs offered on radio and television; the public attitude on various social issues. We even found that some banks had blocked off entire sections of the city from consideration for loans. We found evidence that little consideration was given to the needs of handicapped people.

Fact-finding was interesting and helpful in shaping and changing attitudes, especially the opinions of those who made the studies. It also was an effective way of getting the attention of the community. The following were some of the results for which these intergenerational fact-finding missions were partially responsible:

• The employment of more ethnic guidance counselors in the public schools.

• More bus stops in a neighborhood of apartments for the elderly.

• The lowering of the cost of funerals, and a change in the choice of funeral directors by members of the congregation. We found that for the same casket and service one funeral home charged almost twice as much as another home less than three miles away.

• A much improved relationship with the police and fire departments. In contrast to what others have found in some cities, we received wonderful cooperation; and the departments were very responsive to our suggestions. We also tried to help them by taking on several monitoring responsibilities.

- More basketball leagues, recreational opportunities and musical events in public parks.

Although our fact-finding was not always complete and often was not scientifically controlled, I recommend similar projects as a first step toward community service and political involvement for those over sixty-five in local churches. One positive by-product was our increasing awareness of the many positive public services our city provided for senior citizens about which we had no knowledge before our survey. Many of our members became involved in public volunteer work because their fact-finding made them aware of needs that they could help to meet. Many changed their political views when they came to see conditions for themselves. We found a carry-over from local fact-finding to national political issues. Many persons who entered feeling that the government should not be involved in providing human services came away converted to a new opinion.

• Oral and Written Histories

Rootlessness in a highly mobile city is one of the causes of social and family unrest. There seems little connection between many segments of the population because they don't adequately know one another and may actually appear threatening to one another. Those over sixty-five are uniquely qualified to bridge such gaps. They can be the historians because their common memory can recapture the past. So much of what could be valuable and helpful to the community is often forgotten and put aside. Often feelings are hurt, battles fought over again, some people needlessly ignored, isolated and hurt simply because no one knew the history or the need. As everything is now fed into a computer, and as recordkeeping becomes increasingly complex, harried public servants often don't know what the policy used to be and have little first-hand knowledge of neighborhoods. So much that is wrong in our society has evolved from an institutional depersonalization of public services. For instance, one of our limited income housing developments demanded a children's playground without realizing that the city had provided one just three years before that had already been wrecked by vandalism and overgrown with weeds. We were able to get a new playground with the understanding that the community police it and make provision for voluntary upkeep themselves.

Whether you live in the city, in the suburbs, or in a small town, those over sixty-five "know" much vital information. They have the common memory. We encouraged our people to record their life experience in three ways:

(1) To make a community guide book listing all the services available. This can be an ecumenical project done in cooperation with other churches and agencies. The book should list every support system, agency and service available and the sources of financial and recreational support. The project can be updated every year.

(2) To write the history of one's church or organization or community. (One church I served published the history of the community from colonial days to the present in a 450 page book. This project is still serving that town twenty years later.) At our city church, those over sixty-five developed a three part history of our mission and ministry: a written history, a history in photographs, and a history on tape.

(3) Most valuable of all is the writing of one's own history for children and grandchildren. I persuaded many parishioners to write down their stories or to record them on tape. They had lived through the most interesting period in the history of humankind. Those that tried, found that they were involved in one of the great experiences in life: "I am so glad you pushed my mother to write her story—it's just like a wonderful song. And it has been so good for her to sing it."

Many people can write things on paper that they would find hard to express orally. It allows communication with children and grandchildren without embarrassment. Values which should be shared, that seem "preachy" in conversation, become powerful in a book of written history. Such a project also helps the person involved to recapture some of the joys and accomplishments of the past. Often past happiness and joys are pulled into the present.

Karen Horney, the great psychologist writes in her book **SELF ANALYSIS:** "I have often told my patients that it would be ideal if the analyst merely played the part of a guide on a difficult mountain tour, indicating which way would be profitable to take or to avoid. To be accurate one should add that the analyst is a guide who is not too certain of the way himself, because though experienced in mountain climbing, he had not yet climbed this particular mountain."[18]

The writing of one's life story can be a constructive self-analysis. When Alex Haley's search for **ROOTS** became contagious, many people found that they discovered a part of themselves in those "old-time stories of the past." Personal history is the trustee of so much that is good that it should not be set aside. If it were available, few people could resist reading the life story of their own grandmother or great-grandfather. People who take the time now have a chance to communicate with those who will live a hundred years from now.

I love to give away books. Among those I most frequently give away are 'blank books' in which a person can record his or her own life story. One byproduct of keeping a diary is that it establishes a monitoring operation. One man said to me: "Since you got me keeping a diary, I've learned how empty my days have become. I get up, watch television, eat, walk, read, talk to my wife, do errands, and watch more TV. I've got to get to work doing something more worthwhile if I'm going to keep a diary. What can you suggest?"

Life comes alive when we look carefully at it. It slips by when we aren't looking. When we monitor it intensely we learn that living doesn't always have to be deferred and limited by the values and abilities we slipped into during childhood. Every one of us, regardless of age, can expand our values, our abilities, and even our horizons.

• Cultural Possibilities

Our small city has an especially strong cultural base: a fine art museum, a science museum, an historical museum, an armory, a living museum of the 18th and 19th centuries, Old Sturbridge Village, and many good libraries. We have ten colleges and universities, two community orchestras, two resident theater companies, and an active group of artists, sculptors, potters, and craftspersons. A new civic center brought national artists and sporting events weekly. Like almost every other community, it is a good place in which to live, but too many people over sixty-five are not fully aware of its cultural opportunities and sometimes are not confident enough to take advantage of them.

One of the best things our church did was to canvass the various cultural organizations to find out what types of volunteer services they needed. Almost every one of them is supported by some volunteers from our membership. These volunteers naturally spread the word concerning what is available.

These volunteers do so many different things—driving the children's railroad train at the science center, scaring the children at the museum's haunted house during Halloween week, conducting tours at the art museum, playing in the various orchestras, singing in the choruses and acting in plays, coaching at the Y's and Boys' and Girls' Clubs, guiding at Old Sturbridge Village, working with Boy and Girl Scouts, and sharing craft ability at fairs and art shows. Our over sixty-five members make a major contribution to the community, and the helping experience is as good for them as it is for

56

the city. While this particular city had especially good cultural opportunities, most communities have some. Those in more rural
areas may have even greater need for volunteer support.

• Social Issues

Anyone who accepts Christ as Lord and Master has to be concerned with matters of peace, justice, and righteousness. We might
not all agree on an exact definition of justice, but every one of us can
agree that social justice is a goal Christians can affirm. There is a
Christian perspective which is valid for every part of life. Christ has
a word on racism, hunger, neglected children, battered women, oppressed people, nuclear energy, gun control, capital punishment,
conservation and the environment, drugs and alcohol, abortion,
birth control, matters of war and peace, and the treatment society
gives the weak, the elderly, the young, and the poor.

Those over sixty-five are often forced to relate to the social problems of society in a personal and pressured way. They are more
vulnerable to neglect, for they need more services, and often have
less money to pay for them. Crime feeds off their weaknesses; wars
kill their children and grandchildren. They are more likely to have
poor nutrition and need more medical service. They stand in need of
more police and fire protection. No other segment of society has as
much to lose from inflation and social neglect as do those over sixty-
five.

Those over sixty-five are becoming more active in politics and
social concerns. Maggie Kuhn inspired many of our members to
work actively on the issues that affected them. Her books are essential tools for any church group interested in political action. One
man over seventy wrote to me: "My activities supporting those who
stand for peace make me feel good about myself for the first time in
years. It's the first really unselfish activity I've been involved in for
a long time. I can remember when it was just assumed that
Americans would stand for that which was right. I'm working so I
can feel that way again."

A second area where those over sixty-five seem to reach consensus
concerns the poor and neglected in our society. Many of the elderly
are also poor and left out of the mainstream of society. An even
deeper reason follows from a fundamental change they have observed. Always before in the history of the world, a privileged and
affluent minority stood above an underprivileged and poverty-
stricken majority. Now in America, and in much of the western
world, an overwhelming change has taken place. An affluent and
privileged majority now stands over a poverty-stricken and under-

privileged minority. The psychological damage for that minority, constantly reinforced by the media's presentation of what it considers the "good life," is apt to be far more debilitating than was the case when the majority of people were poor. Those over sixty-five have seen the change in expectations, attitudes and values. They have seen the great depression. They have seen affluence beyond their earlier dreams. They have compassion in a deeply personal way for the "left out," and not a few of them are angry.

One woman said: "I always work harder when I'm angry. I even feel angry when I pray these days. How can we not be angry when we are surrounded by so many Christians who don't seem to care about what is happening to the weak and the poor?" Another who worked actively to influence politicians said: "Can't people realize that the world is now too complex for us to settle for just helping people one by one. Unless we get politically involved, there is no way we can hope to help many people, or solve any of the major disasters that surround us." "Thirty-five years ago," said one man, "while I was in the service I decided that to judge anyone by the color of his skin was wrong. Racism today disgusts me because it is so stupid. A lot of people are like Rip Van Winkle. They've been asleep for twenty years."

Another who decided to spend her retirement years fighting for less privileged senior citizens exploded to me: "I don't want to hear you talking about the future all the time, any more than I want to hear you talking about the past. I'm alive right now, and for all I know I'll be dead tomorrow. I may never make it into your future. My generation cannot wait years for things to change, for adequate medical care, good places to live, for enough to eat, and for someone to care. If we don't get the things we need and the respect we deserve now, we will never get them. It makes no sense at all to talk about the future. We can't wait."

With her, and many like her, I experienced an interesting role reversal—they were doing the pushing and the preaching and I was trying to catch up. They insisted that we give priority to the needs of older people. They supported legal aid for senior citizens, meals on wheels, and all community services which met the needs of the weak. Our church took an advocacy roll for those over sixty-five. Older members would no longer accept the patronizing attitude which had so often been their experience. They were no longer patient with churches or ministers who looked on them as elderly people who need to be "cared for."

All of us, not just those over sixty-five, need adequate medical services and hospital care. A great many Americans do not have access to such care. Nearly forty years ago President Truman sent a national health bill to Congress. Yet there is still no program in place, and medical and hospital costs are now nearly a hundred times more expensive than they were at that time. On November 19, 1945, the President asked Congress for "national compulsory health insurance." "Under the plan, all citizens would be able to get medical and hospital service regardless of ability to pay. The basic points were:

1. Prepayment of medical costs through compulsory insurance premiums and the general revenues.
2. Protection against loss of wages from sickness and disability.
3. Expansion of public health, maternal, and child health services.
4. Federal aid to medical schools and for research purposes.
5. Stepped-up construction of hospitals, clinics, and medical institutions under local administration."[19]

Although similar legislation has been submitted many times, no program has yet been passed. Many older adults have medicare but there are great inequities among states, and many people are incompletely covered. I visited people over sixty-five who denied themselves adequate medical care because they felt they could not afford it. Our involvement taught us a few things:

(1) **The church can be a center of continuing education with the power to change people's minds.** Those over sixty-five have much they can share with others. They can share how it feels to be retired, to experience the frequent deaths of family and friends, and to lack an adequate income. They can tell what it is like to stand in numerous lines, to fight isolation and chronic ill health. They can share the frustration of trying to circulate in a society built for cars when you can no longer drive. They can report what it feels like to wait for a late social security check. As a center of continuing education, the church can be the forum our society needs. Those who have felt the pain are the best teachers.

(2) **No political defeat need be permanent.** We failed many times in our efforts to get real changes made. But no defeat ever lasts long. It really means nothing except that you have the chance to begin again. Although we might be angry when we fail, that anger is constructive if it pushes us to try again. We often learn more from failure than from success.

(3) **Bible study remains the best way to confront people with social concerns.** The Gospel speaks clearly about responsibility, justice, discipleship and compassion.

(4) Today most social problems are systemic, inherent in the very fabric of our society. They can no longer be faced with a simplistic expectation that a charitable attitude and a few loving deeds will bring change. Until the structures of society are politically changed so that justice and righteousness are its primary virtues, the unfairness all around us will continue. The elimination of war, racism, economic and political injustice, and environmental pollution will only come through a political process based on informed citizens who are courageous enough to risk action to support their beliefs.

CHAPTER V
SERVICES NEEDED BY THOSE OVER SIXTY-FIVE

Those over sixty-five need exactly the same services as any other age group. Ironically these services are best provided by those over sixty-five themselves. Experience brings the sensitivity and the empathy which allow a person to respond to human needs with understanding and love. Almost everything in this chapter is borrowed from a report on what I learned from those over sixty-five. Their needs include:

   (I) Spiritual Growth

  (II) Caring Services

 (III) Housing

 (IV) Recreation and Entertainment

  (V) Counseling and Pastoral Care

(VI) Continuing Education

I. SPIRITUAL NEEDS: Every person needs an ongoing devotional life, including opportunities for regular worship, prayer, Bible study, and varied opportunities for discipleship and mission.

In planning a worship program the pastor should make sure that those over sixty-five do not feel forgotten. Pastors are, for the most part, younger than sixty-five. While all clergy try to be sensitive to the needs of the total congregation, life experience can be a limiting factor. If the pastor lives in a family, if he or she has young children, if he or she is thirty-five, then much of the worship program may be subconsciously geared to meet the pastor's subjective needs. It is important to make worship an inclusive experience. Specifically:

(1) Both men and women over the age of sixty-five should have a regular leadership role in public worship.

(2) The content of the service should reveal an awareness of the needs of those over sixty-five. The content should also reflect their blessings and celebrations.

(3) Care should be taken that all ages feel comfortable with each element of worship: the inclusion of popular and familiar hymns, care that language and practice in worship reflect neither agism or sexism, care that sermons and prayers not neglect the experience of whole segments of the congregation, and care that feedback be obtained from those over sixty-five, as well as other age

61

groups. We developed a questionnaire which encouraged people to evaluate our worship as a whole, and each part in particular. Specific questions were asked about every aspect of worship.

(4) Worship should not be simply a spectator activity for those over sixty-five. It must be planned so every person may participate:

(a) In the service itself the congregation should be consistently involved. I once dropped the responsive reading and a litany from the regular service and received the following complaint from a member of the congregation: "Don't you realize that that is the one portion of the service that is truly ours. Many of us can't sing anymore, so we don't enjoy the hymns as much as we did, and we don't hear as well any more, so the sermon doesn't mean as much, but we can read and pray." With that in mind, we purchased pew Bibles and read Scripture lessons in unison or responsively. We found a very high rate of participation among those over sixty-five.

(b) We gave a great deal of continuing attention to acoustics. Even the best worship service is not sufficient if it cannot be heard. Individual hearing aids were provided for all that desired them and a great deal of money was spent improving the sound system.

(c) Efforts were made to insure that our preaching included lay and clergy persons over sixty-five on a regular basis.

(d) We made certain that every person had physical access to the sacrament of communion. A place to sit was provided for those who had difficulty kneeling.

Worship leads to discipleship and mission. Any call to mission should be sensitive to the real strengths and gifts of all worshippers, including older members. Sometimes the call for service is so general and assumes so much, that older people feel unwanted and unneeded. They may feel excluded because the talents called for (both financial and physical) may be those they no longer possess.

Bible study, important at every age, becomes even more essential for those over sixty-five. Many of our experienced members, after much struggle, have learned the right questions. They begin to put behind them the natural human tendency toward hypocrisy and embarrassment. The resultant honesty makes Bible study exciting indeed. We found several things helpful:

(1) We organized the Biblical curriculum thematically as well as chronologically. Those over sixty-five were vitally concerned with

certain themes and were better served when these topics were traced through the books of the Bible. They were less interested in classes which concentrated on one book or one section of the Bible.

(2) Courses from six to eight weeks in length (one class each week) met their needs better than ongoing classes that demanded forty weeks of consecutive attendance. Frequent health problems, visiting family members who lived in other communities, and the necessity of occasionally having to care for loved ones confined to the home, made it difficult for many over sixty-five to regularly attend church school every week of the year. Many could plan to attend each session of a six or eight week course. It was frustrating for them to fall behind in an ongoing course. Even if one does miss a class or two in a short term course, there is the reassurance that another opportunity will begin in a short time. Such a format allowed us to offer a great variety of themes and topics over a single year.

(3) We found that those over sixty-five appreciated a variety of teachers and a variety of course offerings. For instance, a class of older men might enjoy the vitality of a younger person as a teacher. At the same time, many of our people responded best to teachers of their same age group, feeling comfortable in the common experience that bound them together. Classes which used the same lesson material (updated of course) year after year showed greater attrition than those classes that occasionally changed the type and approach of the material.

(4) There was a positive response to self-taught groups with no designated teacher. The teaching responsibility rotated from one group member to another according to a regular plan. With each member reading the same material and feeling responsibility for the whole, exciting learning experiences occurred.

(5) Some classes preferred a series of outside speakers on topics of spiritual interest. Ecumenical and interreligious leaders were also appreciated. A local Rabbi taught a very popular course on the Jewish faith.

(6) Retreats of two or three day duration proved an excellent way to approach serious Bible study and personal devotion. Retreats tended to break the "sameness" of day-to-day living and allowed moments of spiritual self-discovery. Outside teachers of great excellence could be called upon for retreats. Retreat facilities needed to be chosen with care.

(7) Homework was important. Many older people have the time and the interest to do serious daily study. Many materials (large

print Bibles and books, cassettes, and video-cassettes were especially helpful to those over sixty-five.

Several people visited eight to ten individuals each month for the purpose of meditation, devotional reading, and mutual prayer. Intercessory prayer for others was a continuing emphasis. Many people had their own prayer lists, often calling their partners on the phone at an agreed upon prayer time. Many of these visitors were over sixty-five themselves. The sacrament of communion was frequently shared in the homes of shut-ins. A prayer meeting was held at the church every Thursday evening. A majority of that group were over sixty-five, and they formed a nucleus of spiritual power which often energized our entire fellowship. Every person in need knew that intercessory prayer was being offered for them corporately every Thursday and by many individuals each day.

Many people were "yoked" in an informal "buddy-system" in order that they could be mutually supportive to one another on a daily basis. They remembered their special friend in daily prayers and with regular personal contact (either on the phone or by a visit). They reported any special needs to the church if additional help was needed. One woman reported: "I feel that Esther is my security blanket. She is always there and she is praying for me and fills my life with love."

Many persons over sixty-five need help getting their thoughts off themselves. One said: "The past has taken hold of me like a vice. All I think about, all I worry about, happened forty or fifty years ago. I have to escape myself and my memories if I'm going to be of any use to anyone." Another person claimed that she was "devoured by worries about my body." "I finally realized that my body was always making demands on me—that it was getting all my attention. I am going to try to give equal time to my soul."

Such a resolution is not easy, but resources are available. "And He said to me: 'My grace is enough for you, for power is perfected in weakness.' So it is with the greatest gladness that I boast in my weaknesses so that the power of Christ may pitch its tent upon me. Therefore I rejoice in weaknesses, in insults, in inescapable things, in persecutions, in straightened circumstances, for whenever I am weak, then I am strong" (2 Corinthians 12:8-10).

Paul believed that one could rejoice in weakness. Perhaps in the years after sixty-five a person is better able to get beyond the "busy" to the "essential." It may be that we need a consciousness of how weak we all are before we can appreciate Christ's spiritual power. Christ promised that we could start anew at any age. I may fail this time, but the comforting word is that I have started, and that I can start again. It is possible to struggle too much for spiritual strength. Old age can be the time when personal ambition is no longer in the way. With humility, we can finally accept the fact that hardly anything really depends on us. The mature person, who for years has lost spiritual battles because of pride and selfishness, is finally ready to stop the self-deception. Failure still comes, but it is no longer necessary to blame others. We can be honestly sorry, look for further guidance, and try again. As pride recedes, spiritual power finds unoccupied space. A pure heart, unencumbered by selfish desires and unworried about security, apart from Christ, is the first step to spiritual fulfillment.

I noticed that when persons learned to make creative use of their hours of solitude they began to bring order and gain mastery over their lives. As long as hours of solitude hang heavily enough to elicit self-pity they will be destructive, but as soon as they are embraced as hours of devotion and self-improvement, the same hours will build spiritual character and happiness:

- they will build integrity—a discovery of self.
- they will build gentleness and set aside fear.
- they will build frugality, enabling one to be generous.
- they will build a loving spirit, including the acceptance of self.
- they will build humility, allowing increasing dependence on Christ.
- they will build faith, revealing a trustworthy God.

II. CARING SERVICES: The church needs to care for all its people and give serious attention to all human needs including food, nutrition, sexual adjustments, physical and financial emergencies, transportation, visitation, health care, legal aid, and family counseling. At any point of need the most important service the church can provide is the loving care which will meet that need. Almost every church tries to meet the needs of its members; however, some churches do not make those over sixty-five feel warmly welcome and are not institutionally sensitive to the amount of quiet despair which so many of them suffer.

Those presently retired are members of a generation that was taught self-reliance as a primary virtue. They are apt to struggle alone for as long as humanly possible, often finding themselves in the midst of personal tragedy before they call for help on their own initiative. The first challenge of ministry is to build an effective early warning system which will allow delivery of the caring services in time. Only parish visitation and shared experience can build the trust that encourages requests for needed assistance and pastoral care.

It is crucial that the church form a regular contact system which treats each person equally. Otherwise it will be subject to the "illness syndrome." If the infirm and lonely are taught that the physically ill get much better care and greatly increased service, they will quickly discover the "blessing of illness"! If a church is large, it will have dozens of people who realize that good health is a danger which will condemn them to loneliness and isolation. Consequently they are smart enough always to have something physically wrong. The church that does not systematically care for all its older people breeds chronic hypochondria. Since they are so honest with themselves, policies which force those over sixty-five to compete for services and attention can result in serious psychological difficulties.

Meaningful work brings a sense of fulfillment and concentrates one's attention away from one's own difficulties. By far the healthiest and best adjusted group of people in our church were those over sixty-five who were regularly involved trying to help others.

(1) Food and Nutrition: A vicious circle surrounds many older people: they stop eating well and the lost energy complicates their health problems. They lose interest in eating because they don't feel well temporarily. They have decreased caloric needs, depression, memory problems, difficulty with transportation, a disinterest in cooking without a spouse to share meals, or low income. When balanced meals fail to be maintained, nutritional defects develop. Since older people often eat many meals in fast food restaurants and use many canned foods at home, their intake of salt is unusually high. Because of poor nutritian, congestive heart failure and hypertension, common medical problems of the elderly, become very difficult to manage. In addition, chocolates and desserts become favorites of the elderly because they are easy to store and purchase. They furnish little but calories and destroy the appetite for more nutritional foods. A *Washington Post* article of August 9, 1973, reported: "Supermarket managers have told me that many of the heaviest dog food buyers are not pet owners, but the elderly poor who can't make it on fixed incomes or food stamps when they are lucky enough to have either. So they buy dog food, mix it with ketchup, sprinkle on some onions and make a meal of it."

We have already noted how difficult it is to purchase single portions in the average supermarket and how expensive it is to prepare balanced meals for one person. The church has the responsibility to care for the hungry in its community. Each person needs at least one hot meal every day. Volunteers can organize the home delivery of hot meals for shut-ins and a program of noon-time lunches for the

66

mobile. We were able to participate in a food service which offered a fine meal for fifty cents. Of course, a person who could not afford the fifty cents was not charged. There are federal government grant programs which will fully or partially subsidize such a delivery system. Many older people enjoyed preparing and delivering meals. Communication was substantially improved as a result of almost daily contact. The social value of gathering for a daily meal should not be underestimated. Many other values are enhanced by combining recreation (dancing, games, singing, etc.), entertainment (movies, speakers and other programs) and health services (blood pressure tests, health screens, etc.) with a common meal. These meals and related events provided opportunity for meaningful friendships to be established.

(2) Sexual Adjustments: Common stereotypes aimed at those over sixty-five have been most destructive in the area of sexual needs. Although individuals have greatly different drives and desires, the fact remains that a significant majority of those over sixty-five have sexual needs and wish to express their love through sex in exactly the same way as people of other age groups. Assuming the availability of an interested and interesting partner, the majority are sexually active.

Tragically, society paints images of "dirty old men" and asks: "Why doesn't she act her age?" Older persons may be ridiculed for romantic behavior. Images of sexual impotence are psychologically destructive. If the older adult sees himself or herself as "burnt-out" and beyond love and desire, a great part of what is good and wonderful in life recedes into the past and an attitude of self-pity is difficult to avoid.

The church, in its teaching and preaching, in its theology and its ethics, bears a great responsibility for the negative stereotypes which society has developed surrounding sexual activity. Ministers often find it easier to be judgmental than to be caring. Some pastors are unable to listen to an honest expression of sexual need. A few have served over thirty years in the ministry without realizing their own vulnerability and insensitivity. Their preconceived and announced prejudices often prevent honest communication and deny them many pastoral opportunities.

In the area of sex, pastors have a primary and basic reponsibility to listen. A person compromises his or her ability to minister if any parishioner is discouraged from discussing any area of human concern. As my parishioners began to trust me, I was able to see how often they wished to speak about sex and how much at the center of their existence their sexual life, or their lack of a sexual life, happened to be. The pastor can easily have prevented such discussion by inserting his or her own feelings too soon or by diverting the conversation to other areas. I feel that it is the pastor's job to try to help others find fulfillment in every area of life. Ministers have an unequalled opportunity in their sermons and in teaching forums to more clearly express the Biblical view about sex. Sex is a gift from God which deserves celebration and reverence; and as the most intimate expression of love (the greatest of Christian virtues), a person's sexual life deserves respect and recognition for its importance.

(3) Physical and Financial Emergencies: Spiritual life includes every part of living. No ministry can honestly limit itself to spiritual concerns alone. If we are to care about a person's soul, we must also care about that person's health and welfare.

For many over sixty-five, physical and financial emergencies come together. Most people can take care of their financial needs as long as they are healthy, but most are likely to have financial problems soon, if they have health problems very long. It is a myth that subsidized health insurance covers most medical expenses for older Americans. "Medicare pays for only forty-five percent of older people's health expenses; the balance must come from their own incomes and savings, or from Medicaid, which requires a humiliating means test."[20]

In a time when health expenses can quickly accumulate to more than $100,000 for a single illness, a medical emergency can threaten every area of a person's life. The challenge is so overwhelming that it requires political action. Only when society as a whole takes responsibility for the health of all its citizens and treats them all equally according to need, can we be fair with those over sixty-five. They are vulnerable in so many other ways, biologically and psychologically, that in this area where devastation can strike out at any time without warning, they need our help. How many $100,000 illnesses could you or I stand? I believe that the churches of America must take public leadership demanding care for those who can no longer care for themselves.

It is possible that individuals can solve other financial problems in private ways, but the health problem is too large, too out of control, and too unpredictable for most individuals to handle. Some people now sell their homes conditionally making an agreement to give up their property at death in return for a guaranteed lifetime annuity and the use of the home until death. It is also possible that the church or other charitable institutions might be the vehicle for such help. The church should be the front line of defense for older people in emergency situations. Often we:

- initiated contact with the federal, state, or local agencies from which help was available, walking the person through the paperwork involved, providing transportation, and personal support.
- contacted family members and made physical arrangements for health care of other needed services (visiting nurse, home sitting, etc.)
- helped financially.

We built a relatively large discretionary fund in the memory of a Deaconness who had served the poor in our parish with great distinction and self-sacrifice. Spending the interest only, we were able to build a substantial income which provided enough for many to preserve independence and self-respect.

We were often agents of reconciliation and peace between people (family members) seriously angry with one another. We became family for those in need. When an emergency occurred, we visited daily, waited in line, gave transportation, ran errands and did all those things a family would do. For those who did not have families we assigned one layperson and one minister to serve in such a role during the emergency. We also provided daily spiritual backing through intercessory prayer, communion and counsel.

(4) Transportation: Before I lived in the city I never realized how difficult it could be for those over sixty-five to get around in a society based on the automobile. The trolley tracks had been torn up, and public bus transportation had been cut to a minimum on weekdays, and to almost nothing on weekends. Inflation had become so severe that many could not afford to own automobiles. Parking costs alone could be prohibitive in the city. Insurance costs in major cities can be extremely high.

The loss of independent mobility is a critical problem for many because it affects so many other parts of life:

- access to social events
- access to family and friends
- access to medical care
- access to shopping (even access to food)
- access to recreation, entertainment and cultural events
- access to worship and other church activities

Transportation needs have to be met if those over sixty-five are to obtain other essential services. Although this might seem to be an easy problem to solve, we were singularly unsuccessful in meeting the need. We could recruit transportation for an emergency, of a short-term basis quite successfully, but rarely were we able to provide regular, on-going transportation to worship or to other events over a long period of time. Gracious people would take up the responsibility, but within a predictable period, family pressures would force them to ask for relief. There were just too many people that needed transportation. We tried to solve the problem with buses, but with the exception of Sunday morning worship, that solution was not practical. We also had a few heroic people who often made two or three trips to every event, but they could not meet the massive problem.

The only thing that did seem to work was the development of mutual friendships, when people naturally seemed to like each other. When friendships developed, transportation was not a burden. We tried to match individuals with others of compatible natures in the same neighborhood. This method worked many times but still people were often left without adequate transportation support.

(5) Visitation and Friendship: Nothing is more important to the healing process than visitation and friendship. I could furnish a hundred examples of people who were revitalized after forming a wonderful friendship. There is an inseparable unity of the physical body and the human spirit. Christ is called the Savior from the root word "salue" which means healer. Because his shared love has the power of healing, Christ often takes a spirit that has been broken in body and makes it well again.

It is the Christian mission to facilitate that process. Regular visitation (backed by telephone contact) is crucial in all types of healing ministry because the experience of love positively effects the well-being of any patient.

Two of our ministers spent six months grouping our parish geographically into cell groups. Each unit had fifteen families. We thought that such a system would insure that adequate care and constant ministry would take place. The plan did not work for two reasons. First, we attempted the program before the parish was ready to support the plan. Secondly, we assumed a willingness to serve and a benevolence of attitude which we had not yet developed. We had observed what a group of marvelous, fully motivated volunteers could do, but that attitude of loving services had not yet been transferred to our entire congregation. We had not realized that friendships must develop naturally and are not primarily based on geographic or neighborhood boundaries.

I still believe that such a congregational organization is necessary, because old age can be an experience of terror without the support of loving friendships. All people need friends—someone to listen, someone to care—and every person needs to be a friend to others. The church can be a community of listeners who care enough to share the hurts of others. I pray that we can build sufficient spiritual strength to form friendships across generational, educational, cultural, and economic barriers.

(6) Nursing and Hospital Care: At any age, most people will occasionally need special health care. This is often a traumatic time, full of worry. This can be especially difficult for a person over age sixty-five, for that generation grew up in a time when far more illnesses were treated at home by general practitioners, and the hospital was seen as a place where people were sent to die. It is difficult for them to think of the hospital in any other way. They need reassurance based on new attitudes expressing personal care for individuals on the part of clergy and health professionals.

A great part of our work involved helping people over the hurdle of hospitalization and nursing home care. The doctors and nurses who were members of our parish were of immeasurable help. Surgeons who never made house calls would occasionally visit with an older person in his or her home to bring a word of reassurance. Nurses would call patients on the phone at our request and patiently answer all of their questions. Often we were the advocates of the patients. Some doctors look upon the physical difficulties of the aged as "irreversible" or "chronic" while others treat those over sixty-five as they do every other patient with sensitivity and hope. We often helped people who were told that they were "incurable" or "senile" or "chronically infirm" to change doctors and saw that they often made dramatic and persistent improvement with a physician who tried to help. Sometimes we were able to absorb anger which was meant for others. Some people who were negative with everyone else were able to relax because of the patience of our visitors.

One woman was helped many times. We physically moved her without charge from one apartment to another three times, but nothing was ever right. She criticized her volunteer helpers. They were not quick enough or careful enough. When in the hospital, she verbally attacked her doctors and nurses to a point where everyone ignored her. But one of our volunteers continued to love her through all these difficult experiences. That patient love finally broke through and changed the unhappy woman's attitude and behavior.

Sometimes lost memories resulted in trouble. One woman gave her false teeth to one of our ministers so he could get them repaired. The dentist visited the nursing home and reported that her gums were no longer strong enough to accomodate her false teeth. Since her memory often failed, everytime I visited her she would explain to me at length that the other minister had stolen her false teeth. She pleaded with me to get him to return them to her. It is easy enough to be patient with reasonable and fully able people. It was our calling to be patient and loving with those who were continually unreasonable, and who no longer had dependable memories.

I found the work of Vicktor Frankl and Norman Cousins of great value for patients. I recommend giving copies of their books to any person who is ill. Frankl's method of "paradoxical intention" is very valuable for most patients. It seemed to work as nothing else to give them a will to live, to relax them and get them to make the most of the resources available. I saw it enable cancer patients to laugh joyously, not bitterly, and enable heart patients to relax and recover. By pushing the pressures and tragedy of illness to its logical extreme, by getting an image of self which allows humor to wash pessimism away, his method created a climate of healing. His books, *The Doctor and The Soul* and *Man's Search for Meaning*, are especially fine.

I have observed people take charge of all kinds of physical illnesses by means of *paradoxical intention:* "I start to cough, and can't stop so I imagine what it would be to cough non-stop for a week and I get the humor of the situation." "My heart starts to pound and my chest pains and instead of panic, I respond by exaggerating the situation in my mind, concentrating on what a show my body is putting on for the doctors and it relaxes me." "When an attack comes I use 'paradoxical intention.' I decide to concentrate on nothing else, to exaggerate the crisis to its logical conclusions. I even act out in my mind a glorious death scene as if I were a Peter Sellers and the humor always settles me. It is the only way I can escape the chains my physical condition has wrapped around my mind." I am not a logotherapist nor a medical doctor but I can witness to the great effectiveness of Vicktor Frankl's methods in my experience.

The work of Norman Cousins is also extremely valuable. I would like to be able to give every ill person copies of his books *Anatomy of an Illness* and *Human Options.* They are superb statements of the potential every person has to effect healing by his or her own efforts. Cousins believes that every person must accept a certain measure of responsibility for his or her own recovery from disease or diability. He traces the individual's ability to mobilize the body's capacity to combat illness and the power of the human spirit to control the body.

He writes: "Studies show that up to 90 percent of patients who reach out for medical help are suffering from self-limiting disorders well within the range of the body's own healing powers. The most valuable physician—to a patient and to society—know how to distinguish effectively between the large number of patients who can get well without heroic intervention and the much smaller number who can't. Such a physician loses no time in mobilizing all the scientific resources and facilities available, but he is careful not to slow up the natural recovery process of those who need his expert reassurance even more than they need his drugs."[21]

In some instances, Cousins even recommends the prescription of a placebo. The patient is more comfortable with a prescription in hand, and the placebo may even translate "the will to live into a physical reality." There are documented instances of placebos triggering specific biochemical change.[22]

Cousins cites the work of Dr. Jerome Frank of the John Hopkins University School of Medicine. Dr. Frank has observed that the survival rate for persons with heart disease may be just as great treated in their own homes as treated in intensive-care units. Frank felt that the emotional strain of being surrounded by emergency technological equipment offset the gain that equipment offered.

Frank has also shared data on a study in which 176 cases of cancer went through remission without chemotherapy, surgery, or x-rays. There is evidence that those persons believed they would get well and were convinced that their doctors expected them to get well.[23]

Norman Cousins is convinced that a combination of a strong will to live and the happiness resulting from sustained laughter and good spirits lead to his own recovery from a critical illness. His use of laughter, joy, and happy experiences as a spiritual cure for physical illness is worth serious consideration. His books make no excessive claims but present impressive evidence that an ill person may significantly help in the process of regaining health.

I would like to summarize some suggestions and warnings that various health professionals shared with me while I was pastor to so many older persons:

- **The danger of overmedication:** Many older people see different doctors for their multiple ailments, each of whom prescribes medications and dietary restrictions that are often incompatible. Further, those over sixty-five often react peculiarly to drugs; they respond to very small doses or have paradoxical effects. One doctor told me: "I have 'cured' many elderly people by merely stopping all medication."

- **The danger of stopping medication:** "Many successful regimens must be maintained without interruption even while the individual feels well or reoccurrences of the illness, often with entirely new symptoms will appear."

• **The dangers of "unrecognized osteomalacia,"** a result of a loss of calcium from the bone that may be caused by a dietary deficiency: Many of the "arthritic" symptoms, broken hips and crushed vertebra of elderly people can be traced to this loss of bone substance that may have been going on unnoticed for years. A dietary supplement may be needed.

• **The danger of being ever humble and grateful:** Too often help and good deeds are provided more for the benefit of the donor than that of the recipient who is always supposed to show gratitude. Aggressiveness is sometimes needed to make sure that the help is really helpful and notrt of a particular volunteer or an administrative foul-up, serious damage can be done.

• **The danger of intermittent help:** We must remember the past when so often churches accepted the incongruity of letting people go hungry all the year and then serving them Christmas or Thanksgiving dinner. This is even more important where health care is concerned. When critical support for an individual is interrupted by a lapse or absence on the part of a particular volunteer or an administrative foul-up, serious damage can be done.

• **The danger of physicians who are too old:** Margaret Mead suggests that "it's very important to change all your doctors, opticians and dentists when you reach fifty. You start out when you are young with everybody who looks after you older than you are. When you get to be 50, most of these people are 65 or older. Change them all and get young ones. Then, as you grow older, you'll have people who are still alive and active taking care of you. You won't be desolate because every one of your doctors is dead."[24]

• **The danger of the hospital:** Cousins warns that basic hospital sanitation may be inadequate and that the hospital itself is an easy place to catch disease. Hospital routines are often more for the benefit of the hospital staff than the patient. Many people are better when treated at home.[25]

Our most effective visitors, most often over sixty-five themselves, did all they could to make the hospital experience a positive one. They seemed to have a level of compassion and understanding which the rest of us lacked. Every day for five months one of our visitors went to a person who was totally irrational and received nothing but grief in return. He explained to me: "I don't know whether he knows how I feel or not. I don't even know for sure if he remembers my visits, but I remember him as he was and I'll be there as long as he might need me."

There were one or two helpers who fed patients meals and took care of their most intimate needs every day for months. For the most part they received cantankerous rejection instead of thanks. Yet they persisted in love. Since the pharmaceutical revolution in mental health, many people are out in the community instead of in mental institutions. The state hospital released two-thirds of its patients during the years we were in the city. Many of those released lived near the church and needed a continuous ministry. Our church secretary and many others helped them adjust to the pains of a cruel world.

I often thought of the healing ministry of Jesus as it is described in the sixth chapter of the Gospel of Mark. Even those who touched his cloak were healed. I saw several people who were under enormous emotional pressure reclaim a fully healthy life, in part because they had loving caring friends in our church. We never healed people, but in the love of Christ a great many were healed.

(7) **Legal Aid and Needed Social Action:** One of the fundamental changes in the role of the church during the past half century has come in the area of welfare. Once private and religious charities carried the total burden of welfare. Now as a result of the great growth in population and in the complexity of society, private institutions cannot shoulder such a great responsibility alone. The church's role is now more that of an advocate than that of a provider. The church in mission must speak for those who cannot speak for themselves. The words of the gospel are clear. Christ commands His disciples to lift up the weak, heal the sick, seek the lost, and comfort the oppressed. Social action in support of those over sixty-five is especially necessary. When organized, they do have the power and possess the wisdom to be the conscience of society. We found that a taskforce approach aimed at a specific issue, accomplished within a defined time frame, was the most effective way to address problems. Over the years our people were involved in dozens of such activities, about a third of the time successfully. Few projects attempted by a local church result in more effective Christian education than social action programs. If you want your congregation to learn about the Gospel get involved in action ministry. Despite the inevitable controversy about goals and methods such activity usually results in a satisfying experience of ministry for both clergy and laity.

(8) **Family Emergencies:** Few things are more devastating than a death within the family. Serious illness of a family member can be a

traumatic, anxiety producing experience for any person. There are special pressures on those over sixty-five because more emergencies of this nature are likely to occur during that time of life, and individual resources to cope adequately with them sometimes progressively diminish as we grow older. One man who was under the terrible pressure of widespread cancer decided to invest all his energy in helping others. He formed and led a successful blood drive for the Red Cross within our church. He recruited hundreds of people as volunteers and obtained thousands of pints of blood for use in emergencies. Blood was always available to our members because he responded to his crisis with sacrificial service, not self-pity. He told me: "I first had cancer forty years ago. I feel that all the years since have been a glorious bonus, and I still want to make the best of them." Another man, who had made it through a long period of mental illness, dedicated himself to helping others with the same problem. He spent thousands of hours listening, sympathizing, and caring. Many people found full health because of his service and example.

Love is the only effective response to family emergencies. Hearts leap for joy when a loved one smiles, and then, suddenly, a person dies and the smile is gone. It is the responsibility of the church to continue that love and provide the security which love alone can give.

III. HOUSING (including Nursing Homes): Where and how people live can determine to a great extent their attitude toward life and whether or not happiness is possible. Few variables are as crucial as housing.

Every person deserves one place where he or she can feel at home —comfortable, wanted, relaxed, and secure. That feeling is not automatically provided by wealth—in fact it cannot be purchased in the market. Arnold Toynbee, the great historian, makes an interesting observation: "In the painful material contrast between the slums and middle class residential districts there seems to be a redeeming psychological compensation. The higher the income and the better the roofing and the plumbing, the lower the standard of neighborliness. It is well known that the poor give to each other far more spontaneous unremunerated mutual aid than the rich give to each other. Indeed, without a high standard of neighborliness, the difficulties and hardships of slum life would be insufferable. The slummier the slum, the higher the standard of neighborliness is apt to be."[26]

If this is true, and it has not always been true in my experience, it would be worthwhile examining why financial insecurity might bring people closer together. A person feels at home when he or she is really needed by someone else. We belong where we are needed. We feel at home in that place where we have something important to do. Many people solve their problems by plunging into projects involving the home. Housekeeping and gardening and loving care for another person, or even a pet, have produced more healthy and happy people than all medical advances put together. One woman said to me: "I love my home and the little treasures in it. It keeps me sane. I know I'm needed around home. I keep my old clothes on because there is always work to be done. This is the place where I am happy and content." Another woman had two poodles for companions and reacted to those dogs with motherly love: "My dogs do everything that I do. We live life together. I don't know what I would do without them."

A man who lived alone in one room, loved that room more than anything else in life. He would sit quietly, listening to classical music, reading his books, and smoking his pipe. He said: "I like an occasional visit for variety, but I also love being alone here at home. I just fit here. It's not very demanding, and yet I have everything I really want. I can eat downstairs or have a sandwich in my room. It's home to me as surely as any other place I've ever lived."

For many over sixty-five the problem is not as much the physical aspects of "home," although a minimum of financial security is vital in making any place a home, as it is the emotional environment. A person has to feel right about the people and the things that surround life. A home implies intimacy. Every person has the right to choose his or her intimate surroundings. The church needs to be involved in politics to insure that older people can afford to live in safe, secure, life-enhancing places. However, that which is most likely to destroy a "home" is not physical but psychological erosion. A daughter attempts to control her mother's life, insisting on making all the decisions and making the older person feel like a prisoner, neither free nor of great worth to anyone. A son insists that his father sell the homestead "now that mother's gone" and it is "too much for you to take care of." I believe that those over sixty-five should retain all their decision-making options just as long as possible. No one, including the minister or their church friends, is as likely to know what is best for them as they are themselves. Sometimes children, feeling guilty because they have neglected their parents, disguise that guilt in a frantic effort to care for them by controlling their lives. The contrast is bewildering. A person who hasn't been that interested or concerned now tries to make every little decision. The church can help older people feel at home:

(1) By furnishing continuing contact with persons living alone. Regular visitation and phone contacts are necessary. A person living alone can turn on a special light at the same time each night to signal a friend that everything is all right and that nothing is needed.

(2) By furnishing support services needed by those who live alone —shopping, repair work, transportation, recreation, etc.

(3) By helping them (if they wish) find roommates or housemates when they are no longer able to live alone. (Most psychologists find that people are happier shaping their own environment than when they are under institutional care.)

(4) By helping in matters of safety. With the help of senior citizens we offered a security check free of charge. We followed a check list that would help make the home secure from burglary and internal danger. We found exposed and decayed wiring, easily opened windows, deficient or non-existent locks, unsafe apartment buildings, and numerous building code violations.

(5) By helping those living in the same neighborhood or apartment complex get together for mutual self-help and support. A group of people can solve problems no one of them can handle alone. One group of senior citizens living in the same apartment building purchased a large industrial freezer-refrigerator and pooled major food purchases. They had fun doing it as well as obtaining significant financial savings.

(6) By providing needed spiritual services in the home including communion, mutual prayer support, frequent telephone and home visitation contact, and the sharing of cassettes, books, and records.

For a small minority of those over sixty-five the day arrives when they can no longer live on their own and some type of institutional care becomes necessary. Usually this is a nursing home. This can be a time of despair and anguish. If the move has not been based on free decision, and this is often not possible, then the person involved may feel betrayed and abandoned. Most feel like an "outsider" when they enter an institutional atmosphere.

Unfortunately most nursing homes are homogeneous environments without the presence of young adults and children and without a program which involves most of the residents in useful work with people of younger ages. Some nursing homes have smells and sounds that are initially repulsive. Maggie Kuhn calls them "playpens" which keep the aged safely out of the way of the rest of society. She writes; "They're very safe. Playpens are meant to be safe and comfortable. The people are out of the way. A group of gerontology students visited the Southern California Leisure World. Some went in with high expectations of finding paradise—Eden. One World they studied has ten thousand units. It's completely self-contained, with guards, a moat, barbed-wire fences, a hospital, clinics, club rooms, even a community church. The students were concerned about the isolation, but they noted that some residents found it highly suitable and liked the life style."[27]

Nursing homes in their present form did not exist fifty years ago. In 1935 all of New York state had only 28 nursing homes and 441 beds.[28] They now are found over every other turn in the road because:

(1) There are so many more people over seventy-five.

(2) The homes the average family can afford are much smaller today.

(3) Government benefits and public attitudes make it easier for children to ease parents out of their homes. Many financial benefits are not received if a person is not in a nursing home. Our public laws encourage care in institutions rather than family settings.

If it becomes necessary for parishioners to enter a nursing home, we believe that they must:

(1) **Be kept as active as possible.** It is especially important for them to be working on projects they choose and like to do, for them to eat in a common dining room, and for them to be fully dressed each day.

(2) **Be as involved as possible with other people both inside and outside the nursing home.** We held many common parties and celebrations to get natural friendships started. When one of our members had to enter a nursing home, we initiated a period of intense involvement with them. Not only were they visited regularly, but we tried to bring them to events and worship at the church, out for rides, and to recreational and entertainment events that they enjoyed.

(3) **Be encouraged to continue positive activities or hobbies that they had previously enjoyed.** We developed opportunities for Bible study and continued volunteer service within the home. Even those confined in nursing homes can carry on an effective and needed telephone ministry. We paid for private phones for several people who "worked" for us. They had time to give and we had good uses for that time.

In an attempt to help people make positive adjustments we tried to get nursing homes to allow some personalization of rooms. Our experience indicated that personal photographs, beloved objects, and furniture give the nursing home room a sense of home and reminded even the severely demented of valuable memories. One may simply need a chair, ottoman, table (with lamp, box of pencils, hair brush, etc.), or familiar paintings to recreate in the nursing home the setting used for so many years in a person's home. Nursing home life may then act to orient rather than to disorient the resident. One woman loved to show me the albums of newspaper clippings and photographs that she had made of her children. Another had a favorite chair "that just fits me, my moods, and my tendency to snooze." A man who loved to build furniture when younger was surrounded by things he had made himself. He would caress the finish of his roll-top desk and be reminded of wonderful memories. It is not enough simply to criticize nursing homes, for they are "home" for thousands of people who need understanding and love. **There is no nursing home that cannot use the help of a church.**

Those in nursing homes need special attention at the highpoints of the year. Thanksgiving, Christmas, Easter, and other national holidays can be days of greatest loneliness and sadness, for they are full of memories. Every Thanksgiving and Christmas morning, I tried to visit every person in the hospital and attempted to organize visits for those confined to nursing homes. The anniversary of the death of a spouse or a child or the birthdate of a deceased spouse tend to be important times and pressure points for the confined person. No one's own birthday should ever be forgotten. The church can help organize "family-like" responses to these special days.

IV. RECREATION AND ENTERTAINMENT: Every church has a significant responsibility for recreation and entertainment. Those over sixty-five have special needs for they are likely to have less money and less freedom of movement than younger people. The church should be that fellowship in which hope is nurtured and joy discovered. Old age can be that period of life in which people endlessly repeat what they have always done, resulting in boredom and stagnation. One man said: "I fall back on doing over and over again what I have always done. I watch television, go to the movies once a week, and take walks. Every day is like every other." It would be true to say that our church was the recreational and entertainment center for the vast majority of its active members. We planned together what few of us could have undertaken alone.

(1) Entertainment: When all the social groups, circles, fellowships, classes, and organizations were considered together, the church provided its older members with many varied centers of entertainment, all under their own control. Many of their activities focused on mission and social service, but these were also forms of entertainment. The money-making projects were usually great fun. All those who had artistic or craft talents were busy preparing for fairs and bazaars all year. Most of the work teams had regular times of fellowship. Most often they would be held in a different home or apartment with refreshments and socializing as well as work. Even the work projects with youth, at the prison, in the nursing homes, and in the community had elements of entertainment and recreation. Many recreational events (eating out at restaurants, family night suppers, parties, and celebrations) and regular meetings had missional purposes. To ensure the involvement of people who might be left out, we established a network which gave personal invitations to many inactive or single individuals.

(2) Vacations: The church was the center for many group vacations. Some groups intentionally raised funds so that every member of the group could go on a trip. These were from one day to three weeks in duration. Some trips to foreign countries were planned three years in advance to allow time for raising sufficient funds and for study time so we could be absorbed in the culture we were to visit. Often we would plan to visit the work of one of our missionaries. Trips took us to: Cape Cod, the White Mountains, the Coast of Maine, Washington, New York, Montreal, Quebec, and overseas. When possible, we tried to mix generations on trips, so that older and younger people got to travel together.

A good many older story tellers had the most appreciative audiences of their lives. Our trips were always tourist class, or lower—we were primarily interested in people and cultures, and we didn't care for fancy comforts. Our inexpensive trips met the needs of our people. Those who were most affluent often quietly helped with the expenses of the rest, most often without anyone, even the recipients, knowing they had been helped. We made our own travel arrangements, and staff members paid the same rate as anyone else. We were often able to travel at less than half commercial costs. We chartered planes and made our travel arrangements with wholesale travel brokers, often in the foreign country itself. Essentially we had no overhead expenses. The fact that we could fill a bus for almost all our local trips assured the lowest possible costs.

(3) Sports: Our church had bowling, basketball, volleyball, ping pong and all sorts of table games in the building. Many of our best league bowlers were over sixty-five and a great many more were active in the general sports program, providing supervision, coaching, officiating and transportation. Several over sixty-five swam daily together in a downtown pool. At the Y.M.C.A. league the majority of the spectators cheering for our youth teams were often over sixty-five years old. Sports and exercise helped keep the physical body strong for spiritual concerns. Many churches are not fortunate enough to have such fine facilities in the building itself, but cooperation with community agencies can bring similar benefits.

(4) Social Events: The church sponsored a great many social events each month from sweetheart dances, to public issue debates, to forums for political candidates. In an average year there would be five social events each week, except during July and August. Many began with a common meal followed by musical presentations, speakers, movies, or another type of program.

(5) Music and the Arts: Our best programs and the most appreciated by those over sixty-five were musical performances. Older adults were not only spectators but often performers. Our church was blessed with two people of genius, both combining great musical talent and organizational ability. Together they filled each year with fabulous productions. LeRoy Hanson, our full-time Minister of Music, was a wonder! He enhanced the life of our congregation with the majesty of classical and popular music. Far from discriminating against those over sixty-five, he involved a large number of them as performers and choir members. They helped at every stage of his productions and as a whole were his most appreciative audiences. Every year there were many traditional events (A Round-the-Table Sing, a Tenebre Service, a combined concert, shared concert, concert-choir exchanges, and popular music festivals). There were normally two classical evening concerts and at least one major classical work during our Sunday morning worship. In addition to his several choirs, he directed small groups, a bell choir, quartets, instrumental music, and combinations thereof.

The other musical and organizational genius was George Jordan, a unique resource who should have been on Broadway for he had the calling of a great professional producer. Instead, he volunteered his talent to his church in staging musical productions, and coordinating the talents of several hundred volunteers. These projects raised a great deal of money, much of which went to support community projects beyond the church. George made many people feel good about themselves because he involved them in a spectacular event. Each of his productions lasted more than six months. Often "retired" people would work much more than forty hours a week for George, and the entire parish was warmed by the good feeling which came out of every project. It is important to note that his work was entirely inspired, produced, and carried out by laity.

We were also fortunate to have several professional artists in our congregation. Those interested in the theater provided the direction, make-up, staging and talent for several exciting plays. Many fine artists and craftspeople shared their talents by teaching others how to make beautiful and useful things. A few people over sixty-five moved into lucrative second vocations when they learned a craft at church.

Music has been called the language of the gods, and at our church it certainly displayed great inspirational properties. It gave us the feeling of creation, the sparkle of vitality, and the elements of faith. Music and dance, as well as all the fine arts, are the most majestic celebrations of God's glory. For many centuries the finest in all the arts came out of the Christian church. In the past two hundred years some of this heritage has been lost. Those over sixty-five found an ecstasy in living made possible by the arts. When the great choir filled the sanctuary the past, present and future joined as one moment.

(6) The Media: A great many people of all ages surround themselves with electronic input. Trivia from every souce are filling our lives. With the added dimension of cable television, video-recorders, video home projectors, home computers, records, and tape, there is no limit to the choices available.

In 1920 most people had only three major options for private entertainment: playing musical instruments, reading books, or playing table games. Certainly these options are still major activities, but they occupy much less time in the home. An opera or a symphony can come into one's home at a turn of a dial or the touch of a button. Television, with all its mediocrity, now offers an incredible array of choices. Thanks to cable and tape, infinite expansion is possible, bringing quality programming to every hour of the day. The church can help in three ways:

(a) It can spotlight excellence. In the past religious leaders have often tried to censor people while ignoring the far more important task of celebrating quality and excellence. There are many magnificent movies produced each year, some more to the point of the Gospel than many sermons. Theological discussion is often appropriate after a movie or a television program. Some of the best moments of learning take place in a discussion after a shared cultural event.

(b) It can make a movie, a television show, or a cassette the center of classroom experience. Movie cassettes and discs make it possible to bring the preachers and teachers right into the classroom giving unusual stimulation to learning and assuring an entire class a common experience.

(c) It can use the media to proclaim the Gospel. Religious broadcasting has too often let the media control the content of the Gospel message, presenting bland and "safe" messages that would neither stretch the mind nor the heart of the listener. Not enough use has been made of the media to proclaim the Gospel, and almost no attempt has been made to communicate the Christian faith through serious drama, music or art.

V. COUNSELING AND PASTORAL CARE: I have spent many hours with people over sixty-five discussing some pressure that they hoped I might relieve. At the beginning of my ministry I learned I could not be an "answer person," able to give solutions to all the problems people brought to me. I wish I had a wand like Jimminy Cricket in PINOCCHIO because I would have gladly shared the power of a bright star. I found that the problems of most people did not lend themselves to simplistic solutions.

Those over sixty-five experience all the anxiety and pain of every other age. Many of their problems are real—based on the facts of their lives. They are often under severe financial pressures, caught in serious illness, or under the pressure of depression. Their problems are not imaginary which makes them easier to diagnose and much more difficult to resolve. The comments which follow are intended to help pastors and volunteers working with the elderly.

It can be dangerous to exert too much authority in a counseling relationship, particularly because many people are quite ready to yield to and follow the will of a counselor. They are willing to shift responsibility away from themselves and cling to another person if they feel that they can trust him or her and sense they can find either an answer to their problem or the power to escape their difficulty. Frequently much talking on the part of a person in need can be a smoke screen which prevents significant revelation of self. They have learned, since childhood, to use words, often non-stop, as a defense against their own fears. A Christian counselor has less pressure to find "right" answers since both the client and the counselor ought to realize at the start that, although the counselor might have some advantages in training, they both find their power elsewhere from the same Lord and Savior. The counselor does not solve problems by applying his or her special wisdom, but by accepting the other person completely, loving and caring for that person, and by mutually appropriating the powers which Christ promised.

- ## Crisis caused by depression and isolation

Persons over age sixty-five are under pressures that are likely to result in depression. They face sequentially, or all at once, the heaviest burdens of life. Experiences of grief and loss occur several times a year and often involve those persons most precious to them. Older people often despair over the loss of some physical capacity (eyesight, hearing, sexual potency, mobility, strength, energy, etc.) or the loss of some social and personal status because of an almost inevitable erosion of personal power, wealth, importance, influence, and self-esteem. Often left alone and sometimes forgotten by friends and family, they have the most difficult task of managing for themselves at precisely the time of life when they are least able to do so. Such people often seek out their ministers feeling that no one cares about them. One man told me: "No one ever comes into my room to talk to me. I feel that I could die tonight and not one person would pause. I feel I am not wanted . . . I feel that everyone who cared about me is gone, and I wonder, what am I here for?" His feelings and despair are typical of moments experienced by almost every older person.

It is not necessary to "apply" Christian teaching or theology to such a feeling. A warm, caring, patient listener will eventually find that the shared love which is mutually developed will lead to the source of the Gospel. A person who finds love will come alive. A person who finds a meaning in life will not despair. That discovery is not easy and is not always possible in the midst of great anxiety; but love can bring hope, even in the midst of suffering.

It is more important to communicate the love of Christ than to talk about it. If the feeling of love is communicated, it will be contagious. No minister can do it alone—that is why so many others are needed as loving, caring contacts for those in need. Love takes time and involves many little acts of service, affection, and celebration.

- ## Crisis caused by insomnia and illness

Insomnia afflicts many of those over sixty-five. Sleep studies indicate that with increasing age there are fewer hours spent in deep stages of sleep. I was quite surprised to find how many people, otherwise quite healthy, had their energy drained by a lack of sleep. I found once again, that Vicktor Frankl's methods were most helpful. "Insomnia patients often report that they become especially aware of the problem of falling asleep when they go to bed. Of course, this very attention inhibits the sleeping process and helps to perpetuate the waking state. Paradoxical intention can also be applied in such cases. . . . Dubos, the famous French psychiatrist, once compared sleep to a dove which has landed near one's hand and stays there as long as one does not pay any attention to it; if one attempts to grab it, it quickly flies away. . . . The hyper-intention to fall asleep must be replaced by the paradoxical intention to stay awake."[29]

Serious physical illness always has the potential of causing serious emotional difficulties. Fortunately doctors are fully aware of this possibility, and most are able to help their patients move beyond points of emotional crisis. The church must realize that physical illness makes any person quite vulnerable. Any such person needs the reassurance of love, continuing friendship and care. A special pastoral care program might be activated when a parishioner becomes ill. A support structure which has several layers (the pastors, lay visitors, neighbors, special friends, and family) can help the sick person make a more rapid recovery.

• Crisis caused by grief and bereavement

The common wisdom is that time is the great healer so that after a while everyone adjusts, and all grief passes. Such an expectation just isn't true for those over sixty-five because:

(a) They face the death of their loved ones with accelerating frequency. Before sufficient time has passed for grief to be worked out, another period of bereavement sets in.

(b) They are often grouped in a living pattern (in retirement cities, retirement homes, housing for the elderly) which segregates and isolates those most likely to die. They lose new friends as well as contemporaries at an alarming rate.

(c) They are less able to turn to repression because of constant negative stimulus and reinforcement. They are not as likely to be pre-occupied by work and in the business of living.

Fortunately the resources available for working through grief and bereavement are correspondingly strengthened for many people after sixty-five:

(a) **Faith in the Christian hope of resurrection. Studies show that those over sixty-five are twice as likely to believe in personal survival after death than are those in their twenties.**

86

(b) An attitude of thanksgiving for the long productive lives of their contemporaries.

(c) The frequent feeling of relief that a contemporary who has suffered through a long illness is now at peace. For many death is looked upon as a release.

(d) A feeling of responsibility for others. They have strength to give those they love and those who depend on them. Filling this need becomes a role that they discipline themselves to handle.

(e) Many have put aside easy solutions and have learned through experience to trust God, even though few claim to understand the workings of His world.

• Crisis caused by the fear of death

In his fine book, *The Psychology of Human Aging*, D. B. Bromley writes: "There are at least four reasons for the apparent decline with age in late life of anxiety about death. First, through a gradual process of learning the older person has reorganized his thoughts, feelings and motives to bring them into line with the now familiar fact of personal mortality. Second, he may be out of touch out of sympathy with the modern world; hence his personal involvement and future time perspective are much reduced. Third, the ratio of the costs to the benefits of staying alive becomes increasingly adverse and the net value of his personal existence diminishes. Fourth, the process of disengagement diminishes the external pressures or incentives to stay alive."[30]

Nevertheless, almost everyone has difficult moments when death is much on the mind. The fear may range from a belief that the individual is punished for sins in an afterlife, a dread of suffering in the process of dying, or the fright of slipping into an eternal nothingness.

Our society has tried to hide this anxiety by ignoring all evidence of death. We try to make the dead beautiful; we replace simple language with euphemisms (we don't die but "pass away"); and we isolate the dying in institutions. In his extensive study of society's view of death, *The Hour of Our Death*, Philippe Aries traces a progressive attempt to diminish death's potency by removing it from view. This evolution which has changed the way we look at death from a time when it was society's most public act, with memorable death bed scenes to the present antiseptic hospital isolation where almost everyone dies alone is a fascinating and suggestive pattern.

Some people are not as afraid of death itself as of the pain, the agony, and the destruction of dignity which have become part of the process of dying. I rarely meet people who are in terror about an afterlife. People have little interest, to use Harry Emerson Fosdick's phrase, "in the furniture of heaven or in the temperature of hell." Those who share the Christian hope do so based on the resurrection of Jesus Christ and a belief in the trustworthiness of God, without any belief in a magical process of immortality or any thought of being able to scientifically explain what might happen. Their faith sustains them; and they trust God to be a fair and loving judge, just as they would trust a mother or a father to judge their own children in love.

Fear is more likely to be focused on the unknown or a response to the impersonal process of our institutions which transform a human being into a statistic. Almost every person fears the threat of non-being: there is agony in the thought that life might end in complete and empty nothingness. The Christian message of hope is extremely important. At the same time, those who are ill need to be protected from the depersonalizing force of some caring institutions. The pastor and church volunteers can do much to help.

VI. CONTINUING EDUCATION: A person may spend years in study, gaining experience, wisdom, understanding, and knowledge only to find that retirement does not utilize these hard won and unique gifts. Every church can be a center of continuing education with special emphasis on theological and devotional subjects. Many members of the faculty and of the study body will be over sixty-five for this is the group with the time, the talent, and the experience. Curriculum offerings can be adjusted to the experience and interests of available teachers.

There is no artificial limit to the achievement of a retired person. "In a superb example of later life creativity Benjamin Dugger, arbitrarily retired science professor was hired by the Lederle Laboratories, where at seventy-two years of age he discovered the life-saving antibiotic Aureomycin. The profits from the sale of this contribution to medicine amply repaid this pharmaceutical company for its enlightened personnel policy."[31]

There is an excitement in both learning and teaching. The author of Job said it for us (12:12): "Wisdom is found in the old and discretion comes with great age." The collective memory of those over sixty-five is a vital resource which will be totally lost unless efforts are made for preservation. One of our most successful projects was that of a taped memory bank of those important insights, facts of history, and personal experiences which had premanent value. We would interview those willing to record their life experiences. Then that interview was available for members of the family and other interested persons.

Equally exciting are intergenerational learning experiences when many age groups study together. A single age group is often confined by the prejudices, the fads, the emphases, and the trivia which change every few years. Many topics, particularly in the liberal arts, come alive when a class leaps through the horizons of a single generation. Music, theater, politics, government, history—in fact all cultural pursuits—all need the stimulus of the long view. The Beatles follow Bach as naturally as Eugene O'Neill follows Shakespeare, as John Irving follows Jane Austin, as contemporary films build on James Joyce.

It is impossible to seriously study any intellectual discipline without falling into theological and spiritual questions. Theology is too often defined narrowly. Its purpose is to bring us to view God in the perspective of His creation and to put under the Gospel of Jesus Christ the activities we observe in the world. Dietrich Bonhoeffer wrote that the Church should be "Christ existing as Community." The mission of the church is to bring the world into conformity with the way of Christ. As individuals find their minds and souls being formed in Christ, they cannot avoid the responsibility of action and study. It is impossible to look responsibly at politics, at history, at psychology, at any social issue, without getting involved in serious theological investigation. Romans 12:2-3 offers interesting guidance: "And be not conformed to this world but be transformed by the renewal of your mind, that you may prove what is the will of God, what is good and acceptable and perfect. For by the grace given to me I bid every one among you not to think of himself more highly than he ought to think, but to think with sober judgment, weighing according to the measure of faith, which God has assigned him."

I found that those over sixty-five had the vitality and the wisdom to take the lead in such educational programs. They also had the need to participate. Many people surprised themselves with their ability. They had the chance to make a real contribution not only to their church and to history but to the coming generation. In many smaller communities, such projects might be organized on an ecumenical or community wide basis.

CHAPTER VI
THEOLOGICAL QUESTIONS

Now that old age is a much more common experience, more people are asking theological questions about that part of life. More people are becoming sixty-five each year than at any other time in history. The media report stories of aging and ageism. Political action groups are seeking out older people as a carefully defined constituency, and more commercial ventures and media advertisements are aimed at the senior citizen. Those over sixty-five stand in increasing danger of becoming targets of many with vested interests. The church is the one place where they should be able to find respect, integrity, and a quest toward the right questions and truthful answers.

The record has not always been encouraging. The church has allowed the funeral service and funeral customs, an omnipresent experience for those over sixty-five, to become both artificial and sentimental. The church often isolates its older members and treats them as problem people who need custodial care. Sometimes the church seems more interested in their wills than in them. One man said: "I have attended more than a hundred funerals and I have noticed a real difference between the funeral service and Sunday worship. Funerals seem to avoid life while Sunday worship seems too involved in life. Why can't you ministers be honest?"

Another rightly concluded: "People must think I'm fragile. Often they talk about me instead of to me when they are in my presence. They will censor whole topics because I'm there. What can I do just to be treated like a person?" Pastors could begin by admitting their own vulnerability. We can confess our own ignorance, doubts, wounds, and weaknesses. No one will be very surprised. I found that a real relationship begins with honesty. My weaknesses, at times, became sources of strength. Those over sixty-five are willing and able to give a helping hand to those in trouble. I believe that a great many of my successes came because of apparent failure. As I review my ministry, I see many times when I made serious misjudgments, overreacted, or was just stupid. Members of the congregation recognized that I was wrong, but because they loved me, they made things right. That attitude was typical for senior citizens.

• At Peace With Oneself

Many people look for peace in their lives and are surprised that they never seem to find it. The only peace which any of us can find is peace with ourselves. No matter how much security we seem to have there are always things that are unfinished and incomplete. We have unrealized goals, unfulfilled dreams, and tangled relationships. The events of life make suffering and struggle inevitable. Christ taught risking our lives for His sake is the only way to find life! Older people are on the cutting edge of life every day, sometimes not even recognizing the risks they are taking. Paul wrote: "The Spirit comes to the aid of our weakness" (Romans 8:26). This is the experience of many people who found peace in themselves even while in the midst of continuing pain and frustration.

An individual can make peace with the self when he or she gets involved with the contagious love of Christ. Often I observed people who came out of the deepest depression and self-pity when they lost themselves in the practice of Christian love. Once a person's focus leaped beyond the self, peace would come, even amidst constant suffering. Stephen Spender wrote a poem which described the struggle of those I knew:

Swear never to allow
Gradually to smother,
With noise and fog,
The flowering of the spirit.

It helps to remember that Christ was a human who went through many of life's pains. He struggled, He was tempted, He was left alone, He was betrayed, He was whipped, and He died.

The power of the Lord is received most often when one is utterly unhappy and dissatisfied with life. When we are lowest in self-pride, Christ begins to speak clearly. I noticed that the poorest and the most humble of my parishioners were often those of quiet faith who were at peace with themselves.

• The Christian Funeral

What should be done when death inevitably comes? Certainly we should approach death with the same integrity with which we address life. If we find life to be filled with wonder and stand in awe of its great beauty and variety, we can carry that faith forward in worship, even in the face of death. If we have found life hard and full of suffering, that reality cannot be denied at death.

Life has to be taken for what it is, a free gift, that we neither earn nor fully understand. To the extent that we are reflective, we know what we like to do, what makes up happy, and what we value. We come to recognize what we admire in others and in ourselves. Those over sixty-five taught me a positive image of Christian life:

• They had a willingness to expend themselves for others. Many wrapped themselves up in Christian mission by getting involved in causes that served people.

• They had a sustaining faith in a God they trusted, who enabled them to live in fellowship with Christ and other people.

• They had the gift of good humor, never taking themselves too seriously, often sharing jokes of self-depreciation, while they took their vocation as Christians seriously.

• They had a sense of the importance of family and friends. They gave top priority to acts of love and understanding.

• They found deep meaning in Christ and in the church. Christ was a living presence. Daily prayer, frequent communion, and worship brought them a personal relationship with God.

This view of life gave them a background through which they viewed death. The initial reaction to the death of a loved one is often a feeling of great and irreplaceable loss. There might also be a sense of relief that a person has escaped from great pain and suffering, or even the feeling that heavy burdens and responsibilities have been lifted from the back of the survivor.

Those who attend a funeral face the problems of grief and bereavement from many different perspectives. Some are devastated, while others may be quietly pleased and even experiencing relief. Others are looking forward to an inheritance. Some are filled with feelings of guilt and an awareness that the opportunity for forgiveness has passed. Others have the sense that they have said all the words which needed to be said. Many might be nostalgic about what might have been. The emotions of those at a funeral are surely complex and difficult to describe, since they are often ambivalent within the same person.

A funeral is a service of worship. The coffin is not a replacement for the altar and, for Christians, the dead body should not be the center of worship. I have found the following guidelines helpful:

(1) The pastoral care of the surviving family members should be the primary concern of the minister. They need to move through difficult days with grace and understanding. The immediate period after death is not a time for theological training. If the family has strong feelings concerning the service, I do not believe the minister should insist on his or her point of view. (The time for teaching is in church school and by means of seminars on funerals. We held such seminars, including visitation to local funeral homes, comparing services, prices, and attitudes.)

(2) Seminars and classes are good places to discuss questions like these:

(a) Why is it preferable to conduct the funeral in the sanctuary of a church?

(b) Why should the casket be closed during the service?

(c) Why should worship at a funeral be honest and direct, avoiding both words and actions which are not authentic? Should the beliefs and the previous activity of the deceased control the service? What about the eulogy?

(d) Should the funeral service include all elements of worship including congregational participation, hymns, and a spirit of praise?

(e) How should a funeral lift up the life and faith of the deceased?

(3) Although we put forward a strong point of view in the seminars, we believed that in the time of bereavement the family should have the power of choice. The minister may outline choices, but an attitude of love and care should always supercede other considerations.

(4) A funeral need not and should not be a time of ostentatious and sacrificial financial expense. Families should be encouraged to budget expenses with the same care and at the same level that they handle their other expenses. We found that an annual survey of costs at various funeral homes was helpful. This helped to alert parishioners to a reasonable price range and tended to keep over-all costs down.

(5) We emphasized those personal acts of love in the life of every person rather than popular images of success. Most people wanted the funeral service to lift up the quality of the life and the faith of the deceased. It is possible to celebrate human life and personal achievements while emphasizing the grace of Christ. The Christian hope is based solely on Jesus Christ. His sacrifice on the cross and the resurrection on Easter symbolize God's gift of eternal life. This grace is celebrated in every service of worship. Our attitude at each funeral was based on Christ's cry on the cross: "Father, into thy hands I commit my spirit" (Luke 23:46). Since God is trustworthy the life and spirit of every person can safely be passed back into the creator's hands. It is the revelation of Christ and the nature of God that brings comfort at the time of death as at every other time of pressure in life. There is no need to depend

on an abundance of good deeds on the part of the deceased. Justification is by faith through grace, shown most clearly by the love Christ gave on the cross.

(6) We visited the family in their home before the initial calling hours so their choices could be made without rush or pressure. If possible, such decisions were not to be made at the moment of death or at the calling hours.

(7) The pastoral care provided in the weeks following the funeral may be more important than the care provided in the time immediately following death. The church family should provide several alternative sources for potential care. Laypersons must share with the clergy in a common ministry to provide caring help. Many of our laypersons, especially those over sixty-five, were of enormous help because they had been through similar experiences themselves.

Many people avoided these problems by working out their own funeral service in advance. In this way the service can represent, in a most positive manner, the faith and witness of the individual. The family is secure in the knowledge that the service represents the will of the deceased. Such preparation should be completed well before a "final" illness. In my experience the planning of one's own funeral service was a most constructive stimulus to intentional living. It helps a person to distinguish between the essential and the trivial in life and to set personal priorities. This also proved to be the best time to consider costs, the feelings of others, and the ethical considerations which reflect a person's values.

A great deal has been written by theologians and philosophers about the meaning of life. The more abstract the thought, the more likely the conclusion will be cynical. In practical experience very few people, who are physically and mentally healthy, fail to find meaning in their own lives.

After long experience I have found only two small groups of healthy people who have not found meaning in their own lives. The first are those few people whose faith in a personal resurrection is so strong that they wish for death so they can rejoin their closest loved ones immediately. Their loss was so great that they didn't want to go on alone. The second group is made up of those who do not feel needed by anyone. They consider themselves utterly neglected and alone. In their isolation they sometimes have little desire for life.

Apart from these two groups, and those who have never been

worn down by physical and mental illness, the vast majority of people find meaning and fulfillment in life. This meaning expresses itself in several ways:

- identification with a cause bigger than themselves.
- being needed by another person or group of persons.
- fulfilling one's personal place in God's creation by becoming the person the Lord intended one to be.
- life in an environment of love and happiness.

Old age is described in Ecclesiastes as the fading light of a winter day, with a threatening storm on the horizon. Without an outward source of power, that judgment is true. For many Christians the power is found in the boundless love of God and by trust in the Lord's essential goodness. Meaning comes when we participate in God's love, as we respond to the needs others have for caring, loving service. This love constitutes the basic rhythm of life.

Christianity is not a faith which promises contentment, peace, or an easy life. Meaning in life is found through a commitment to be part of a community of love. It may be well to remember the word that is read at almost every interment: "Then shall the dust return to the earth. But the spirit shall return to God who gave it."

Throughout the Bible the way to meaning in life is not described as a search but as a process of losing oneself in life. In the great theme of hope in Second Isaiah (55:1-5) God reveals a love as broad and as strong and as deep as the force of creation. The bread and water of life are available:

"Trust in the Lord, and do good; so you will dwell in the land, and enjoy security. Take delight in the Lord and he will give you the desires of your heart. Commit your way to the Lord; trust in him and he will act. He will bring forth your vindication as the light, and your right as the noonday. Be still before the Lord, and wait patiently for him; fret not yourself over him who prospers in his way."
—Psalm 37:3-7a

"The fear of the Lord prolongs life, but the years of the wicked will be short. The hope of the righteous ends in gladness, but the expectation of the wicked comes to nought. The Lord is a stronghold to him whose way is upright but destruction to evil doers."
—Proverbs 10:27-29

"Trust in the Lord with all your heart and do not rely on your own insight. In all your ways acknowledge him, and he will make straight your paths."
—Proverbs 3:5-6

"If I speak in the tongues of men and of angels, but have not love, I am a noisy gong or a clanging cymbal. And if I have prophetic powers, and understand all mysteries and all knowledge, and if I have all faith, so as to remove mountains, but have not love. I am nothing. If I give away all I have, and if I deliver my body to be burned, but have not love, I gain nothing."

—I Corinthians 13:1-3

CONCLUSION

We have shared in this book some of the things learned in a church which served and was served by thousands of people over sixty-five years of age. I came as pastor with the idea that I was sacrificing myself for those who needed my help and ministry. Instead, I was the one who was constantly helped and the one who received ministry.

Over those years I learned how hollow were the success images which I had accepted along with so many other Americans. I found myself surrounded by people who were living in the present. They had put aside the common American experience of living for tomorrow. In a sense they were living in an ongoing Advent season, waiting for Christ to come again and for the Easter morning which would follow.

This book has been their story—the story of working with and for people over sixty-five years of age. First we presented a new view of ministry among this age group. Then we presented a plan for lay ministry in the chapter on the expanded staff. We saw the church as "Christ existing as community" by describing its worship, pastoral care, youth work, Christian education, stewardship, evangelism, mission, and ministry. We looked at cultural concerns and the services needed by those over sixty-five: food and nutrition, sexual adjustments, physical and financial emergencies, transportation, visitation and friendship, nursing and hospital care, legal aid, family emergencies, housing, recreation, entertainment, pastoral care, counseling, and continuing education. This led to reflection on some theological questions.

In each case I have shared what I have learned from people who are often called "old." They taught me much that cannot be adequately described in a book of any length. I wish I had the literary ability to communicate their spirit and their feelings. I remember so many real people who lived the way I would like to live. Their stories express to me better than anything else how one can live triumphantly.

I wish I could record the experience of hundreds more in detail. I remember Grace Pulsifer, who at ninety-eight still told self-depreciating, humorous stories and often laughed at her own weaknesses. Day by day she faced difficulty with grace and forbearance and celebrated her pleasures with joy. Grace obviously loved life and loved to share it. Since she outlived all the members of her immediate family, she lived alone, defiantly rejecting the traditions of society by remaining independent, out of a nursing home. In almost everything she was self-sufficient. When she attended her eightieth high-school reunion I suggested that she might be one of the last "old Yankees." For fifteen years we celebrated each of her birthdays together. I often wondered about her secret. How could she live life without complaint and remain in such good humor? She suffered serious pains from arthritis and other severe ailments. Why didn't she show self-pity? She had lost all her close loved ones and lived alone, thinking daily of a husband and sister who had lived with her for more than a half century. Grace told me that people would ask Ben, her husband: "How is it that you can live so happily with two women?" He answered: "I just keep on the good side of one of them all the time."

Grace was a person of faith and trust. As I observed her life I noticed that she had adopted the basic rhythm of caring, loving service. She was interested in others; she concentrated on the events of the world; she had a contagious sense of humor; and she. was endlessly kind, thinking of the needs of others. She lived each day as a joyous gift from God.

I remember Leon Treadwell. Leon repaired vacuum cleaners and small appliances for a living. When I arrived he was already over seventy and seemed unconcerned about retirement. Every Sunday, he was the head of some thirty ushers who were called "Leon's Legions." He was a quiet faithful worker who gave many hours each week to his church. Though of modest means, he had the natural dignity of genuine success. He was elected at different times chairperson of almost every major board and committee in our church. In a more conventional church a person would have had to be more "successful" in his vocational life to be chosen for the highest leadership positions, but Leon was that rare person whose power was in his personality and his character instead of being vested in his position or his wealth. He was a hard worker whose values and judgments were solid. He was a Christian who was called to ministry in our city. I learned a lot from him—most of all about Christian dignity. I visited him many times in the hospital during his last illness. He amazed me because he spent no time on his pain or personal worries. He insisted on hearing about the church. One day I asked him: "How can you think and talk about other people and the church when you are in so much pain and distress yourself?" He smiled quietly and said: "Don't you understand? All of us are here for awhile. We come and go, but that which is valuable and meaningful persists only to the extent that we care. I believe in the values of Christ, and I am committed to those values with all the strength I have. I know that nothing depends on me, but I have invested a lifetime in those values. They have sustained me many times. I am not going to give up on them now."

He had given a lifetime of loving, caring services for anyone in need; and he possessed a radiant, abundant faith, equal to any pressure. His obituary in the local paper was quite short—a few words about his business, a mention of his church and community service, and the statistics of his family. In the weeks that followed, dozens of individuals, male and female, old and young, but mostly the poor and the weak, told me of the hundreds of little acts of love Leon did for them. He spent his life giving services of love that never got into the newspaper, but were remembered long after front page news is forgotten. There are others who have lived triumphantly in this same way. I pick Leon because he is not alive to be embarrassed. It seems that humility is a part of love too.

I remember Larry and Nita Beliveau who shared with those around them the magic of happiness. Every day for them was one of adventure. They shared a wonderful curiosity and a spirit which exudes fun and good humor. Larry loves animals, children and all kinds of people. Nita loves Larry. He has nurtured and welcomed into his home every type of bird or animal, from a baby lion to a wild turkey. He spends as much for food for his birds and wild animals as he does for himself. He never held a position of authority in our church. He was not elected to any committee, but he was typical of the type of person who would do anything for any other person joyously. Larry is that miraculous type of person who can brighten any room with fun and laughter within seconds, no matter what the crisis. He is just full of life! He delights in you and suddenly you delight in yourself. He feels good, and suddenly you feel good too.

I didn't meet Larry until after he retired, but he had a vitality that was shared by most of my friends over sixty-five, those who were so busy in living that they didn't have time to worry about age. They didn't repress thoughts. Their minds and hearts were full of today's opportunities for love and thanksgiving.

For years my favorite cartoonist has been Bil Keane who draws *The Family Circus*. My wife and four children have brought the same spirit of excitement and happiness to our family that Bil Keane portrays in his family circus. During the week when I was leaving the downtown church for a new appointment, I saw a Sunday cartoon by Bil that reminded me of the church that I would never forget.

The house in which the family had lived for a decade had been sold. The full moving van is ready to roll; a "sold" sign is on the lawn; and the family is walking away from the house. The three older children are each carrying toys: mother, her potted plants; the Father is carrying P.J. and his briefcase. The dog Barfy is carrying a bone. The house is filled with cartoonist's "thought balloons," each containing one of the mother's precious memories: Billy coming home as a new baby from the hospital, a New Year's Eve Party, Daddy coming home with a new rake, images of the mother herself: sitting knitting socks, bandaging a hurt Billy, the arrival of her parents for a visit, Dolly praying beside her bed, a first birthday party, a Christmas morning, the whole family in bed together on a winter's night, arriving home exhausted from vacation, reading to the children, a Thanksgiving dinner, Dolly's first tooth, Daddy bringing a new puppy home in a box; boiling the baby's bottle at night—on and on the memories go. Thinking only of possessions, the father casually asks: "Forget Anything?" Emphatically and sadly the mother answers: "NEVER!"

Our church was such a family. It was made particularly precious because our leaders were those who had lived and loved over several generations. They were experienced in life and in faith. I have so many memories of their love and service. This book has shared a few. "Will I forget what so many over sixty-five did for me and that church?" "NEVER!"

NOTES

1. *The Gerontologist*, April, 1982, Vol. 22, No. 2, "The 1980 Census and the Elderly", Jacob S. Siegel & Cynthia M. Taeuter, page 144.

2. *The Annals of the American Academy of Political and Social Science*, "Planning for the Elderly", July, 1978, "Long Term Care Policy Issues: Alternatives to Institutional Care", Faye G. Abdellah, page 28.

3. *Maggie Kuhn on Aging*, pages 13-14.

4. Robert Butler, *Why Survive?*, page 1.

5. Maggie Kuhn, *op. cit.*, pages 17 and 21.

6. *The Gerontologist*, June, 1982, "The Language of Ageism", Frank N. Nuessel Jr., page 273.

7. Simone de Beauvoir, *The Coming of Age*, pages 343-344.

8. Nadine Stair, by permission.

9. *A Companion to the Study of St. Augustine*, "The Christian Ethic", Thomas Bigham and Albert Mollegen, page 373.

10. Leo Tolstoy, *Last Diaries*, page 43.

11. Eric Erikson, *Childhood and Society*, page 268.

12. Ethel Smith, *The Dynamics of Aging*, page 123.

13. *The Journal of John Wesley*, Volume 7, page 358.

14. Ed. Thomas S. Kepler, *The Fellowship of the Saints*, page 700.

15. Robert Butler, *op. cit.*, page 233.

16. *John Wesley's Letters*, Ed. John Telford, Volume V, page 56.

17. Simon de Beauvoir, *op. cit.*, page 331.

18. Karen Horney, *Self Analysis*, page 14.

19. Harry S. Truman, *Years of Trial and Hope*, page 19.

20. Robert Butler, *Why Survive?*, page 4.

21. Norman Cousins, *Anatomy of an Illness*, pages 55-56.

22. Cousins, pages 55-56.

23. Cousins, pages 133-134.

24. *The New Old: Struggling for Decent Aging*, Ed. Ronald Gross, Beatrice Gross & Sylvia Seidman, "Growing Old In America", by Margaret Mead, page 271.

25. Cousins, *op. cit.*, page 29.

26. Arnold Toynbee, *Cities on the Move*, page 227.

27. *Maggie Kuhn on Aging*, pages 43-44.

28. Butler, *op. cit.*, pages 271-272.

29. Vicktor Frankl, *The Doctor and The Soul*, pages 204-205.

30. D. B. Bromley, *The Psychology of Human Aging*, pages 281-282.

31. Butler, *op. cit.*, page 77.